COVENANT • BIBLE • STUDIES

The Prophecy of Amos and Hosea

Christina Bucher

faithQuest® ♦ Brethren Press®

Covenant Bible Studies Series

Copyright © by *faithQuest*®. Published by Brethren Press®, 1451 Dundee Avenue, Elgin, IL 60120

All rights reserved. No portion of this book may be reproduced in any form or by any process or technique without the written consent of the publisher, except for brief quotations embodied in critical articles or reviews.

Unless otherwise noted, scripture quotations are from the New Revised Standard Version of the Bible, copyrighted 1989 by the National Council of Churches of Christ in the USA, Division of Education and Ministry.

Cover photo: David Radcliff

01 00 99 98 97   5 4 3 2 1

Library of Congress Cataloging-in-Publication Data

Bucher, Christina.
    The prophecy of Amos and Hosea / Christina Bucher.
       p. cm. —(Covenant Bible studies)
    ISBN 0-87178-008-9 (alk. paper)
    1. Bible. O.T. Amos—Study and teaching. 2. Bible. O.T. Hosea—Study and teaching. I. Title. II. Series: Covenant Bible study series.
    BS1585.5.B83 1997
    224'.6'0071—dc21
                                                                                              97-19277

Manufactured in the United States of America

Contents

Foreword vii
Preface ix
1. Amos, a Prophet 1
2. Amos's Message: Justice and Righteousness 7
3. God's Upside-Down Kingdom 12
4. The Prophet as Intercessor 17
5. God's "Chosen" 22
6. No Faithfulness, No Loyalty, No Knowledge of God 28
7. Estrangement, Separation, Abandonment 33
8. Political Infidelity 38
9. God's Compassion 43
10. Reconciliation 47
Suggestions for Sharing and Prayer 52

Foreword

The Covenant Bible Studies series was first developed for a denominational program in the Church of the Brethren and the Christian Church (Disciples of Christ). This program, called People of the Covenant, was founded on the concept of relational Bible study and has been adopted by several other denominations and small groups who want to study the Bible in a community rather than alone.

Relational Bible study is marked by certain characteristics, some of which differ from other types of Bible study. For one, it is intended for small groups of people who can meet face-to-face on a regular basis and share frankly with an intimate group.

It is important to remember that relational Bible study is anchored in covenantal history. God covenanted with people in Old Testament history, established a new covenant in Jesus Christ, and covenants with the church today.

Relational Bible study takes seriously a corporate faith. As each person contributes to study, prayer, and work, the group becomes the real body of Christ. Each one's contribution is needed and important. "For just as the body is one and has many members, and all the members of the body, though many, are one body, so it is with Christ.... Now you are the body of Christ and individually members of it" (1 Cor. 12:12,17).

Relational Bible study helps both individuals and the group to claim the promise of the Spirit and the working of the Spirit. As one person testified, "In our commitment to one another and in our sharing, something happened.... We were woven together in love by the Master Weaver. It is something that can happen only when two or three or seven are gathered in God's name, and we know the promise of God's presence in our lives."

The symbol of these covenant Bible study groups is the burlap cross. The interwoven threads, the uniqueness of each strand, the unrefined fabric, and the rough texture characterize covenant groups. The people in the groups are unique but interrelated; they are imperfect and unpolished, but loving and supportive.

The shape that these divergent threads create is the cross, the symbol for all Christians of the resurrection and presence with us of Christ our

Savior. Like the burlap cross, we are brought together, simple and ordinary, to be sent out again in all directions to be in the world.

For people who choose to use this study in a small group, the following guidelines will help create an atmosphere in which support will grow and faith will deepen.

1. As a small group of learners, we gather around God's word to discern its meaning for today.
2. The words, stories, and admonitions we find in scripture come alive for today, challenging and renewing us.
3. All people are learners and all are leaders.
4. Each person will contribute to the study, sharing the meaning found in the scripture and helping to bring meaning to others.
5. We recognize each other's vulnerability as we share out of our own experience, and in sharing we learn to trust others and to be trustworthy.

Additional suggestions for study and group-building are provided in the "Sharing and Prayer" section. They are intended for use in the hour preceding the Bible study to foster intimacy in the covenant group and relate personal sharing to the Bible study topic.

Welcome to this study. As you search the scriptures, may you also search yourself. May God's voice and guidance and the love and encouragement of brothers and sisters in Christ challenge you to live more fully the abundant life God promises.

Preface

The prophets are some of the most loved characters of the Bible. In part, we love the moral vindication we get out of seeing them serve the Israelites their comeuppance. But the prophets are for our day, too.

The biblical prophets, when read for today, justly criticize us for our lagging faith. Amos and Hosea lived at the economic and political height of Israel, but they prophesied for the endless generations of faithful who, from time to time, wander away from God.

Amos calls out for justice for God's children and creation. He is the one who criticizes our pride and our failure to act justly and kindly toward one another. Hosea berates Israel and us for abandoning God and lacking an inner feeling for God. Not only do we not act, we are alienated and distant from God.

Even after the spiritual flogging they give us, we ought to love the prophets because they assure us that God cannot *not* love us. Their painful message always concludes with the promise of God's love and compassion, giving us new energy to act for and to be reconciled with God.

—Christina Bucher

Recommended Resources

Brueggemann, Walter. *The Prophetic Imagination*. Augsburg Fortress, 1978.
Craige, Peter. *12 Prophets*, Vol. 1 (Daily Study Bible—Old Testament Series). Westminster John Knox, 1984.
Heschel, Abraham J. *The Prophets*. Harper & Row, 1962.

1

Amos, a Prophet
Amos 1:1-2; 3:7-8; 7:10-17

Amos, a herdsman, is familiar with the gross inequities between the rich and the poor; he champions the oppressed. Called to be a prophet in both the political and the religious realms, Amos clarifies his purpose and the necessity of being a prophet.

Personal Preparation

1. In this unit we will be studying the messages of two biblical prophets: Amos and Hosea. When you hear the word *prophet,* what kind of person do you think of? Who speak as God's prophets today? Read Amos 3:7-8. What do these verses reveal about God's relationship to the prophets?
2. Read Amos 1:1-2 and 7:10-17. What do these two passages tell you about Amos's activity as a prophet and the nature of his prophetic message? Why does Amaziah, the priest, tell him to get out of town and go back home? What does the story tell you about what it means to speak as God's prophet?
3. Think about the people you identify as prophets of God in our time. How does the church view them? What does society think of them?
4. When in your own life have you acted or spoken in a prophetic way, perhaps confronting a wrong in your community? Jot down some words that would describe the feelings you experienced. How did people respond to you?

Understanding

A few summers ago I received a letter from a college student who planned to take my fall course on the biblical prophets. Being an unusually industrious student, she wanted to do some reading in advance of the course and had gone to her local bookstore to find books on the topic. When she asked for books on the prophets, the bookstore clerk pointed her in the direction of the business and economics section! With some amusement Karen said, "No, I want a book on p-r-o-p-h-e-t-s, not on p-r-o-f-i-t-s."

Our society cares a lot about making money but little about hearing the truth. Even in our churches, many of us hear little about prophets and prophecy. What we do hear often focuses on the prophets as future-tellers. In the church, we tend to emphasize those prophetic passages that speak of the coming of a messiah. Although the biblical prophets did talk about the future, we misunderstand the prophets if we view them only as predictors of the future. They appear to us more like human Ouija boards or crystal balls than as individuals who passionately confronted the powerful institutions of their time with the word of God.

Amos and Hosea: Two Short Prophetic Books

In our Bibles the books of Amos and Hosea can be found among a group of writings called the "Minor Prophets" (also called the "Book of the Twelve"). This collection follows the four books Christians refer to as the "Major Prophets" (Isaiah, Jeremiah, Ezekiel, and Daniel), and it brings the Old Testament to a close with the book of Malachi. The terms *major* and *minor* in reference to these prophetic books have to do with the length of the books, not the quality or significance of their content. When the Bible was written on scrolls, a Major Prophet filled an entire scroll, while the twelve Minor Prophets could fit together on one scroll.

Several factors make the study of these books difficult. Most of these prophetic books collect the prophets' *sayings* and contain few *stories* about the prophets. (The book of Jonah is a notable exception.) Because of this, we know relatively little about the prophets' lives. Reading the Prophets can also be challenging because the prophets' sayings lack introductions that would tell us something about the settings of the sayings.

Finally, we may fail to recognize how the sayings have been organized by the books' editors. In some cases the editors seem to link units by certain catchwords. For example, a message about justice may follow another message about justice even though the two messages were delivered on different occasions. Another organizational principle comes through, as well: the practice of alternating prophecies of doom and prophecies of hope, usually concluding with a hopeful message about God's mercy.

From Amos 1:1 we learn that Amos was from Tekoa, a town in the hill country of Judah, approximately ten miles south of Jerusalem. From the rest of the book, we learn that Amos delivered his messages in the cities of the

Amos, a Prophet

northern kingdom of Israel, especially at the official religious center at Bethel. Amos also may have taken his message to the capital city of the northern kingdom, Samaria.

Amos 1:1 locates Amos in a particular era. Amos lived during the time when Uzziah ruled the southern kingdom of Judah and Jeroboam II ruled the northern kingdom of Israel. This places Amos in the mid-eighth century B.C. At this time the kingdom of Israel experienced a period of prosperity, although, as we shall discover from Amos's message, there was prosperity for some, but not for all, Israelites.

The prophet Hosea, whom we'll study in sessions six through ten, also prophesied to the northern kingdom of Israel, probably only a few years after the time of Amos's prophetic activity. Hosea witnessed the decline of the northern kingdom and possibly also its defeat at the hands of the invading Assyrian troops.

Amos and Amaziah: Prophet and Priest

Amos 7:10-17 contains the only story we have about the prophet Amos. In this story we read about an encounter between Amos and Amaziah, the priest of Bethel. Amaziah has warned the king about Amos, saying, "Amos has conspired against you."

The priest tells Amos to leave the country and go back home to Tekoa. The story is tantalizingly ambiguous. Why does Amaziah tell Amos to go home? Is he concerned for Amos's welfare? Or, does he want to get rid of a troublemaker?

The evidence suggests that Amaziah is concerned not with the truth of Amos's message, but with the maintenance of order in the kingdom. Amaziah cannot bear to hear that all is not well in the kingdom, and he cannot bear to have the Israelites hear that all is not well. He does not appear to wonder if Amos's message of death and exile may possibly be true. He simply does not want to hear about it.

We can probably all identify with this attitude. Who among us has not avoided confronting difficult realities? We would rather not know that a relationship is falling apart. We prefer not to recognize the warning signs of a dangerous dependency. We say, "Turn off the evening news. It's too depressing. I don't want to hear it." Each of us has been Amaziah at some time in our life. We know him intimately. We understand denial.

I recall hearing a story about a desert nomad who got up in the middle of the night with great hunger. He lit a candle, pulled a bag of dates from under his bed, and began eating. But with his first bite, he noticed a small worm in the date. So he threw the uneaten fruit out of the tent. He bit into the second date and it, too, revealed a worm. The same with the third! Finally, deciding he would see a worm in each date, he blew out his candle—and, in total darkness, contentedly ate all of the dates.

Yes, the darkness of denial often seems preferable to the light of reality. But to be fair, we should recognize that as priest Amaziah was expected to uphold the status quo. Like the prophet, the priest, too, mediated between God and the people. The priestly office, however, was more institutionalized and therefore more open to control by the rich and powerful. Although many Christians speak of pastors and ministers, rather than of priests, we have individuals who perform the priestly functions of maintaining the religious traditions and of officiating at such momentous events as weddings and funerals. It is not an easy task.

You and I: Prophets as Well?

Do we know anyone in our own community who is an Amos? In his book *The Prophetic Imagination*, biblical scholar Walter Brueggemann describes the task of prophetic ministry. He identifies the first task of the prophet as that of *criticizing*. Brueggemann writes that the role of the prophet is "to cut through the numbness, to penetrate the self-deception," and, in doing so, the prophet brings "to public expression those very fears and terrors that have been denied so long and suppressed so deeply that we do not know they are there."

When we are deep in denial, the prophet is the one who demands that we face up to reality, that we admit that our marriage is failing, or that we have a dependency problem. The prophet is the one who forces us to recognize that our economy is in a shambles, our cities are a mess. We should not be surprised, then, when we read that Amaziah tells Amos to get out of town, go home, and shut up. But instead of meekly getting out of town, Amos keeps talking:

> Therefore thus says the LORD: "Your wife shall become a prostitute in the city, and your sons and your daughters shall fall by the sword, and your land shall be parceled out by line; you yourself shall die in an unclean land, and Israel shall surely go into exile away from its land." (Amos 7:17)

Is the prophet then a social, religious, and political gadfly? Is he the one who makes us feel guilty? Is she the person no one wants to have around because she never has anything good to say?

Brueggemann identifies a second task of the prophet—that of *energizing*. A prophet is more than a critic. She is the visionary who imagines alternatives to our present situations of despair. He is the poet who calls us to look beyond the present reality. Prophets urge us to *hope*. And in this way they carry out a pastoral function. I like the way Henri Nouwen, in his book *The Wounded Healer,* describes this pastoral quality that must flow through in any preaching:

> [It] is not merely a skillful use of conversational techniques to manipulate people in the Kingdom of God, but a deep human encounter in which a [person] is willing to put his own hope and despair, his own light and darkness, at the disposal of others who want to find a way through their confusion and touch the solid core of life. In this context preaching means more than handing over a tradition; it is rather the careful and sensitive articulation of what is happening in the community so that those who listen can say: "You say what I suspected, you express what I vaguely felt, you bring to the fore what I fearfully kept in the back of my mind. Yes, yes, you say who we are, you recognize our condition."

In the books of Amos and Hosea, we will listen for both the prophets' criticism and their energy, their grim judgments and their encouraging visions. And in listening to the message Amos and Hosea relayed to the Israelites some 2700 years ago, we will listen for the message they have for the church today. For, as spokespersons for God, they do, indeed, recognize our condition.

Discussion and Action

1. Share the understanding you had of the biblical prophet's role before you read this lesson. Then, discuss the understanding of the prophet you discovered in this lesson.
2. Tell of a time in your own life when you spoke or acted as a prophet. What happened? Have you ever acted as an Amos, speaking the truth to someone who did not want to hear you? Share those experiences in the group.
3. Do you know anyone you consider to be a prophet? Does that person fit the characterization of the prophet as one who both criticizes and energizes?
4. Share ways in which you have been an Amaziah and resisted hearing the truth about yourself, your church, your community.
5. Think about pastors you know. Do they fill the priestly role or the prophetic role described above? Many pastors likely try to serve as both priest and prophet to their congregations. Talk about ways your pastor functions as a priest and ways he or she functions as a prophet.

With which role does your pastor appear to be most comfortable? With which role are you more comfortable?
6. In *The Prophetic Imagination*, Walter Brueggemann writes, "Our culture is competent to implement almost anything and to imagine almost nothing." What do you think he means? Do you agree with his observation? How important is imagination in your life? in the life of your covenant group? What is the relationship of imagination and change?
7. Discuss ways in which the covenant group, your congregation, and your denomination can act as prophets in the world today. Think about some specific prophetic actions (criticizing actions or energizing actions) that you could carry out through this study. Ask people to research the possibilities so you can choose at least one group project next week.

2

Amos's Message: Justice and Righteousness
Amos 5:21-24

Amos's message centers upon the demand for justice and righteousness in the community life of God's people. Our worship of God is meaningless if we do not work for justice in our communities.

Personal Preparation

1. Read Amos 5:21-24. Sometimes when the prophets speak as God's messengers, they quote God directly. Here, the "I" refers to God. When Amos speaks for God in this passage, what actions does he criticize?
2. This session will focus on the concepts of justice and righteousness. Find a quiet moment to sit with your eyes closed. Think about the word *justice,* and allow an image to come into your mind. What image do you associate with justice? Do the same exercise with the term *righteousness.*
3. What kind of worship do you think God desires of you? of your church?
4. How does your congregation's worship relate directly to the life of your community? to the global community?

Understanding

Let justice roll down like waters,
and righteousness like an ever-flowing stream.

Martin Luther King, Jr., must have loved this image of justice and righteousness. Although I never heard the Reverend King speak in person, I have listened to tapes of his sermons and speeches. Whenever I read this verse from Amos, I can hear King's voice ringing out like a church bell calling people to worship.

Justice and Righteousness

The absence of justice and righteousness in Israelite society led to impassioned prophetic pleas and indictments. What do the words *justice* and *righteousness* mean? These two terms appear throughout the prophetic writings. In the Bible, the Hebrew word for justice, *mishpat*, refers broadly to the rights due to every individual in the community. *Mishpat* can refer to the decision rendered by a judge (and the Hebrew word for judge, *shofet*, is closely related to the term *mishpat*). Justice, then, has to do with judgment, and, in fact, *mishpat* can be translated into English as either "justice" or "judgment." (The KJV translates *mishpat* in this verse as "judgment.") From the biblical perspective, when a judge delivers a judgment, justice occurs.

Amos 5:15a instructs the people to . . .

> Hate evil, and love good,
> and establish justice in the gate.

In ancient Israelite and Judean cities, the judges in the community assembled in the open space just inside the city gate. There they would listen to any problems or conflicts that had arisen within the community. Amos, then, was instructing the people to make sure that the judges rendered just judgments. (Amos 5:12 indicates that the bribing of judges was a problem in Israel.)

In his book *The Prophets*, the Jewish theologian Abraham Heschel comments on the difference between the Greek and the Israelite concepts of justice. For the Greeks, justice is balance, as pictured by the scales. Think of our statues of justice in this country (e.g., a woman standing blindfolded and holding a scales in her hand).

Both the Greeks and the Israelites understood that justice includes the idea of fairness, but Amos, in contrast, displays justice as a surging, flowing stream. In this image, justice moves. It has the power to rush forward, to move obstacles in its path. The imagery of water suggests that justice is a life-giving force. For Amos, this image best portrays the dynamic power of justice.

We sometimes confuse justice and order in our society. The Reverend King wrote in 1963 that "the Negro's great stumbling block is not the White Citizen's Councilor or the Ku Klux Klanner, but the white moderate who is more devoted to 'order' than to justice." The search for justice in society can often be messy, disorderly, as the civil rights movement taught us. Amos and the Bible as a whole teach us about justice, not about order.

What does the word *righteousness* (in Hebrew *tsedaqah*) mean, and how does it differ from *justice*? Many people associate the terms *righteous* and *righteousness* with personal piety and a "holier than thou" attitude. This association, in fact, confuses the term *righteous* with the English expression *self-righteous,* a word used to describe individuals who self-centeredly believe they follow God's teaching, but few others do. We have all, no doubt, encountered in our lives at least one self-righteous person. Perhaps we ourselves have even acted self-righteously at times.

Rather than having to do with personal piety, righteousness deals with the interconnection of individual and community. A woman acts righteously when she deals generously with others. A righteous man cares for a needy person in the community. Righteousness, then, has to do with loving kindness, graciousness, consideration, and concern—all characteristics of interpersonal relationships. You've probably heard the expression "Do the right thing." Amos was a "do the right thing" prophet.

No Worship?

The verse concerning justice and righteousness with which we have been dealing occurs within the context of a passage that is rather troubling (Amos 5:21-24). In this passage God declares a lack of interest in feasts and assemblies, a refusal to accept the peoples' sacrifices, and a determination not to listen to their musical praise. Feasts, assemblies, sacrifices, and praise—these were the very substance of the people's worship life! How could God reject their praise and adoration, their worship?

I can remember as a youth arguing with my parents that I should wear the same clothing to church as I wore the rest of the week (blue jeans and flannel shirts), because what mattered was my inner attitude, not my outward appearance. Although my wardrobe has changed as I've aged, I continue to struggle with the question of priorities. When do we become too concerned about image? When do we focus too much on the form of our worship response to God and neglect the justice and righteousness God requires of us?

Although some readers may find in Amos 5:21-24 a call to abandon totally the worship of God in favor of a life of service, most interpreters suggest that Amos here calls the people to reprioritize their concerns. Amos says that God does not care about worship *if* justice and righteousness are lacking in the community. Justice and righteousness *first*. Without them a community cannot truly participate in the worship of God.

Justice and Peace

It's so easy to read Amos and remark, "My, weren't those Israelites awful? The rich oppressed the poor (5:11-12) and lay around drinking wine and taking it easy (6:4-6). They really deserved Amos's wrath." In a Bible study, I once heard a person spurt out indignantly, "But *we* don't have injustice in *our* community." We know from Amos that justice and righteousness were missing in the Israelite towns of his time. If we keep an ear to Amos's words and turn an eye to our own communities, do we not see an absence of justice and righteousness in our own homes, churches, and communities?

My father taught me about justice and righteousness in everyday dealings in our community. I learned from him always to count my change after making a purchase. He cautioned me to make sure that I had received what was due to me—but no more. If I was handed too much change, I learned to return the excess, even though I might be tempted to profit from the clerk's error. The church also taught me about acting justly toward members of my own community. I did not, however, learn a lot about global justice as I was growing up. I heard much about peacemaking but little about the ways in which peace and justice are interrelated.

In his book *The Spiral of Violence*, the Brazilian church leader Dom Helder Camara has written about the connection between injustice and violence. He describes the spiral of violence as beginning with injustice, which often destroys human dignity without involving actual physical force. People required to live in poverty and suffering because of their country's economic policies suffer this "invisible violence." Camara's connecting of violence and injustice calls all Christians concerned about peace to learn also about the establishment of justice in our world.

The prophet Amos speaks to us today, calling us to attend to matters of justice both in our local communities and in the global community of which we are a part. If we strive to act justly and righteously towards others, perhaps God will once more sit back to enjoy "the noise of our songs and the melody of our harps."

Discussion and Action

1. Share the images of justice and righteousness that group members experienced during their preparation time.
2. Talk about difficult images of justice—especially the image of a blindfolded woman holding a scale. Compare and contrast this with Amos's powerful, moving, life-giving force. How would this latter kind of justice change the justice system in our country?
3. Think of examples from your own life of times when you experienced

justice. Have you ever been treated unjustly? Share these experiences with the group.
4. Talk about the qualities that make a person righteous. Do you know any righteous people?
5. Respond to the quote: "But *we* don't have injustice in *our* community!" Where do you have justice in your community? Where do you see injustice? Where do you see people working to create justice in the community?
6. Amos criticized the Israelites for worshiping God without concerning themselves with the life of their community. Think about your own congregation. Do you have a good balance between your worship life and your community outreach? Is there a way in which your covenant group can improve this balance?
7. Does your covenant group need some outreach to balance your worship life together? Plan for a community project that you can do during these next two months. Decide on the prophetic actions you will take as a group. Decide whether to focus primarily on global issues or on local concerns.

A suggestion: Our court systems are commonly called justice systems. Contact a prison chaplain or a police chaplain and learn about his or her work in the justice system. How can your group members participate in these ministries?

3

God's Upside-Down Kingdom
Amos 5:4-17; 6:1-7; Luke 6:20-26

God's justice transforms social inequities. Under God's rule, the first are last and the last, first. This biblical understanding of God's rule as an "upside-down kingdom" calls us to reprioritize our values.

Personal Preparation
1. Read Amos 5:4-17 and 6:1-7. Session one identifies the prophet as one who criticizes. What behaviors does Amos criticize in these passages? Do an "archaeological survey" of your own house—and reread these passages as speaking directly to you.
2. Amos speaks out against economic injustices. What economic injustices do you see in your community? in your country? What behaviors would Amos criticize today in your congregation and community? Make a list to share with your group.
3. Read Luke 6:20-26. Compare Jesus' message with that of Amos. How do these messages speak to you personally?
4. How should the church respond to economic injustices in our society today? Envision some practical responses that would work in your own congregation.

Understanding

I spent eight weeks one summer in New Haven, Connecticut, living in one of the Yale University colleges located in the center of the city. Every day I got up early to walk across the beautiful quadrangles and past the magnificent university buildings. But every morning, as I walked past the church located across the street from my college, I saw a woman about my age rolling up a blanket and preparing to leave her sleeping area on the church steps.

God's Upside-Down Kingdom

She had beautiful eyes. Some mornings I looked into her eyes as we passed and wanted to speak. But I said nothing. Other mornings I looked straight ahead as I walked by, again not knowing what to say. The rest of the day I spent working on my project in the library. But I felt haunted by that woman's eyes.

What toss of the dice created this situation? Why does my sister human being sleep on the steps of a church while I return home at the end of the summer to a comfortable house in a friendly neighborhood? There are some who would say, "She's lazy. Obviously, she prefers sleeping in the streets to getting an honest job." Others would say, "It's not her fault. It's the fault of society. Obviously, she's never had the opportunity to get a good job and support herself."

I don't know who is right. I never stopped to talk with her.

The Haves and Have-Nots

According to a recent U.S. census, there are millions of poor in this country, with children making up a large portion of the poverty-stricken. In developing countries, where there are more than one billion poor, one-third of the population lives in poverty, according to the World Bank's latest World Development Report.

People live in poverty in our world for many reasons. Some have no training and cannot find jobs that pay very much. Others have the training but cannot find jobs in the field for which they prepared. Still others struggle with mental illness or addictions and become homeless. Governmental policies, such as tax structures, can make it nearly impossible for poor people to get out of poverty. And some people live in poor countries where there is a low level of production.

We have limits on our resources, and some countries and some individuals are benefitting from more than their fair share of the world's resources, while others suffer because they do not receive the minimum needed—adequate shelter, food, and clothing.

In the eighth century B.C., Amos preached to a society in which the rich were getting richer and the poor were getting poorer. Sound familiar? In Amos 6:1-7, the prophet attacks the "lifestyles of the rich and famous." These wealthy Israelites lounged about on beds decorated with expensive ivory carvings. They ate meat every day. (Most ancient Israelites rarely ate meat.) They drank vast quantities of wine and used the most expensive oils to care for their bodies. To these "notables" who liked to be first at everything, Amos says, "Okay, you like to be first. You will be first—the first to go into exile when our country crumbles."

In 5:10-12 we read Amos's attack on those who oppress the poor. To those who "trample on the poor" (5:11) and "push aside the needy" (5:12), Amos announces,

> You have built houses of hewn stone,
> but you shall not live in them;
> you have planted pleasant vineyards,
> but you shall not drink their wine. (5:11b)

Throughout the sayings that have been collected in the book of Amos, the prophet criticizes those Israelites who exploit the weak, poor, and afflicted members of their society. Although Israel at that time was experiencing a kind of economic and political renaissance, not all members of society shared in the prosperity of the time. Archaeological excavations have supported Amos's critique of the Israelite economy by revealing that in eighth-century Israel, some families lived in large, expensive houses while others lived in much smaller, cheaper structures. What will such excavations centuries from now reveal about our own rich and poor dwellings?

According to covenant theology, God owned the land, and Israelite families occupied the land as God's stewards. God had given Israel the land so that each family could manage a plot of ground as their inheritance. With the establishment of the monarchy under Saul and David, two centuries before the time of Amos, a new social system had come into conflict with the older system of inheritance. New classes of the wealthy emerged, who had been rewarded for their service to the king by an increase in their land holdings. This, of course, meant that some families were pushed off their land. The loss of land in such a traditional, agriculturally based society led to poverty and starvation.

In response to this exploitation of the poor, Amos speaks out against the wealthy landholders. Conspicuous consumption at the expense of others' needs is wrong. The use of power to gain wealth and social status is sinful. And the valuing of profit over personal relationship is unrighteous behavior. Again, this sounds painfully familiar.

The Upside-Down Kingdom

Amos's message to the wealthy, oppressive Israelites reflects the reversal of human expectations that the Gospels tell us about. In Luke's version of the Beatitudes, Jesus pronounces a blessing upon the poor, hungry, and downtrodden of society, saying, "Blessed are you who are poor, for yours is the kingdom of God" and "Blessed are you who are hungry now, for you will be filled" (6:20-21). To the rich and well fed, however, Jesus offers a warning, "Woe to you who are rich, for you have received your consolation" and "Woe to you who are full now, for you will be hungry" (6:24-25a). Both Jesus and Amos speak about a kind of reversal of status where God takes the side of the poor and hungry over against the wealthy and elite of society. In his book *The Upside-Down Kingdom,* sociologist Donald Kraybill uses the image of the "upside-down kingdom" to describe Jesus' message:

> Things in the Gospels are often literally upside down. Good Guys turn out to be Bad Guys. Those we expect to receive the reward get a spanking instead. Those who think they are headed for heaven land in hell. Things are reversed. . . . The least are the greatest. The immoral receive forgiveness and blessing. Adults become like children. The religious miss the heavenly banquet. The pious receive curses. Things aren't like we think they should be.

"Things aren't like we think they should be." Our society teaches us that a big house and a new car indicate that the owners are successful. But Amos and Jesus chastise the wealthy. Society teaches us that those who are poor have failed. But Amos and Jesus stand on the side of the poor.

Some Latin American theologians refer to the view of the poor found in the Bible as "a preferential option for the poor." In *The Gospel in Solentiname,* the Roman Catholic priest Ernesto Cardenal has collected some of the conversations he had with the poor people of Solentiname, an archipelago in Lake Nicaragua. Cardenal comments that the profound wisdom of these laypeople should not surprise us, since the gospel "was written for them, and by people like them."

In a discussion of Jesus' Beatitudes, one of the *campesinos* (rural people) observes, "A rich person that shares love has to share his goods, too. That's how he shows that he shares love. Because if he says he has love and doesn't share his goods, how are we going to believe him?"

If we Christians say that we have love but we don't share our goods, who will believe us?

Discussion and Action

1. Share experiences you have had (similar to the author's) of being confronted with the injustice of the "haves" and the "have-nots" in today's world.
2. Share the list you made of behaviors Amos would criticize if he were living in the United States today. (You might wish to refer to your personal "archaeological survey.") What do these behaviors tell us about our priorities and God's priorities?
3. Discuss the similarities you found between Amos's message and Jesus' message in the Beatitudes and woes of Luke's Gospel.
4. In his book *The Rich and the Poor*, Mennonite economist Carl Kreider states that Christians must become more aware of the differences between rich and poor nations in the world. Discuss ways in which your covenant group can help your congregation learn more about the local and global economy. You may want to sponsor a special series of lectures, Bible or book studies, or worship services devoted to this topic.
5. Schedule a special time of fellowship for your group and watch the video *Country* together. (Or show the video for those who wish to "stay late" after your meeting.) This 1984 movie, starring Jessica Lange, depicts the plight of a farming family being forced by the government to give up their land. After watching, discuss how the themes in the movie relate to what you have been studying in Amos about economic and social justice.
6. Call a shelter and get some facts and figures about homelessness in your community. Who is homeless? Does the information you have gathered fit your stereotypes of the homeless? Why, or why not?
7. Close by singing or listening to words of the hymn "Brothers and Sisters of Mine" on page 63.

4

The Prophet as Intercessor
Amos 7:1-9; 8:1-3; 9:1-4

The prophet is one who speaks for the people, as well as to the people. In a series of five visions, Amos intercedes on behalf of the people. There are times, however, when even intercession is not enough.

Personal Preparation
1. Read Amos 7:1-9; 8:1-3; and 9:1-4, noting how the prophet speaks to God on behalf of the people.
2. Reflect on your understanding of God. How do you think God responds to human petitions? Can humans "change God's mind" through prayer?
3. Recall times when you have come to God in intercession on behalf of some person or group of people. Are there times when you knew others were praying to God for you?

Understanding

"Intercession is spiritual defiance of what is, in the name of what God has promised," writes biblical theologian Walter Wink in an issue of *Sojourners*. In other words, intercession is a complaint, a lament carried to God that things are not working as planned. I like what Wink has to say, but I also realize that I find it disturbing. I realize that at a fundamental level I think of God as someone totally in control of things. It seems improbable to me that humans might "change God's mind."

Yet, I read the Bible, and I find examples of individuals who argue with God—and win! God appears to alter the divine plan as a result of human intercession. Abraham argued with God about the fate of the citizens of Sodom (Gen. 18:23-33), and God agreed to modify the number of righteous inhabitants needed to spare the city from destruction. (And even when ten righteous inhabitants could not be found, God spared Lot and his family.) Moses begged God not to abandon the unfaithful Israelites (Exod. 33:12-17), and God stuck with the grumbling, complaining people.

Despite knowing these biblical examples of "spiritual defiance," I discover that I have been deeply imprinted with a view of God as all-powerful and unmovable and with a belief that people of faith must simply accept what comes along. As I read Wink's thoughts about intercession as spiritual defiance, I hear in my head, "Trust and obey, for there's no other way."

Believing the Future into Being

Yet far from simply accepting whatever comes along, the diligent intercessor imagines an alternative to the present reality. Abraham imagined an alternative to the destruction of all the inhabitants of Sodom. Although the requisite number of ten righteous people did not appear, God did spare Lot and his family. Moses could not envision a future for the people he had led out of Egypt unless God accompanied them. He pleaded with God and the future was altered. Walter Wink says that intercessors "believe the future into being."

In the past three lessons, we have seen how the prophet acts as God's messenger, speaking God's truth to the people. In today's lesson, we will see another important function of the prophet, that of intercession. In addition to speaking *for* God to the people, the prophet speaks *to* God on behalf of the people. Here is where Amos's series of five visions comes in. These visions in chapters 7—9 have to do with divine judgment. They do not give specific reasons for God's judgment, but we know from the rest of the book of Amos that the Israelites oppressed the poor and needy. This would be one likely reason for God's judgment.

In the first two visions, Amos sees objects that he thinks symbolize judgment. In the first vision, he sees a swarm of locusts (7:1). Because they are able to destroy crops, locusts nearly always symbolize devastation in the Bible. In the second vision, Amos sees a "shower of fire" (7:4). Fire also frequently symbolizes destruction. See, for example, the prophetic oracles in Amos 1—2, where God announces the divine intention to "send a fire."

In both visions, Amos intercedes with God on behalf of the Israelites. The prophet does not offer excuses for Israel; instead, he reminds God that "Jacob is so small." Amos does not question the justness of God's intention, but rather, he asks God to show compassion for this people, who, whether they recognize it or not, stand weak and helpless before God.

Amos succeeds in his intercession. God hears the prophet and says simply, "It shall not be." The destruction will not happen—not because Israel deserves to be spared, but because God chooses to show mercy.

There are three more visions, however, and in these visions we discover that Amos has succeeded only in postponing disaster. In visions three and four, Amos sees a plumb line (7:7) and a basket of summer fruit (8:1). On these occasions Amos does not intercede. Instead, God asks the prophet, "Amos, what do you see?"

After Amos responds correctly, God immediately interprets the visions for Amos. The plumb line "measures" Israel (7:7-9). Because the Israelites fail to measure up, God announces that destruction is inevitable. The envisioned destruction has both religious and political implications: Israelite religious places will be ruined and Israel's royal family will come to an end.

In the fourth vision (8:1-3), a play on words in Hebrew points to the meaning of the vision. The "summer fruit" (*qayits*) indicates that the "end" (*qets*) is near. Sounds of wailing will replace the songs of praise heard in the temple. Death will strike the Israelite people.

The fifth, and final, vision (9:1-4) confirms the message of judgment. Amos sees God standing "beside the altar" (possibly at the central sanctuary in Bethel). God's presence at the sanctuary formerly symbolized divine protection. In Amos's vision, divine presence points to a judgment that will shake the very foundations of Israel's existence as a people.

Do the final three visions of judgment negate the mercy of the first two intercessions? Or, do they indicate that there is a point beyond which even intercession cannot help? Amos did succeed twice in interceding with God to repeal the judgments. That he continued to have visions of judgment indicates that, despite his intercessions, the people continued in their ways. Although God was willing to grant the Israelites the opportunity to mend their ways, the Israelites refused to change.

Knowing When to Say No

One year I had a student who was doing poorly on exams. Near the end of the semester, he came to my office to ask what he could do to improve his grade for the course. I gave him a small lecture on the need to ask for help early in the semester, and, since it was his first year in college, I showed some leniency in my grading. When he again appeared in my classroom the following fall, I felt good, thinking he appreciated having learned something from me about responsibility. To my dismay, he repeated his behavior of the year before. This time I showed no leniency.

Parents, too, learn when to show mercy and when to discipline. We want our children to know that we will always love them; yet, we want them to become responsible for their behavior. When they make mistakes, we may give them a second chance and maybe even a third, but we would be remiss as parents to give them fourth and fifth chances. Parenting guides encourage us to practice "tough love" not because it's fun to say no to our kids, but because our kids need to learn that limits exist. We say no for their benefit.

In the case of the Israelites, God twice relented. But the Israelites did not change their ways. This does not mean that Amos's intercession failed to move God. Amos's prophetic criticizing, however, failed to change the people's behavior. Like a good parent, God practices "tough love."

Above all else, intercessors must possess an enormous amount of hope—hope that God will show mercy and hope that the people for whom they intercede will change.

Although it disturbs my sense of theological orderliness, I want to believe with Walter Wink that intercessory prayer can liberate our world from that which opposes God and God's purpose. Intercessory prayer does not alter who God is. But if we truly live in a covenantal relationship with God, then I believe God responds to my and to our attempts to change our world. Intercessory prayer changes me, changes us, as we imagine a new future into being.

Discussion and Action

1. Begin by focusing on question 2 in Personal Preparation. Share about your understanding of the interaction between God's will and human will related to prayer. How do Walter Wink's ideas about the function of intercessory prayer fit your understanding of who God is and how God relates to humankind?
2. Discuss a key point in this lesson: intercessory prayer asks both that God alter the divine plan in response to human need and that we humans change our ways. Can you name times when prayer has appeared to change the circumstances? or when praying has changed you?
3. Tell about when you have been involved in intercessory prayer—either as the one praying or the one receiving prayer. In either case, how do you determine the "effectiveness" of intercession?
4. Christians do not always incorporate intercessory prayer into their worship life. In what ways do you want to see intercessory prayer included in your private or family devotions? in your covenant group devotional time? in congregational worship?
5. Look for examples of intercessory prayers in your hymnals or worship resources. Make a list of the individuals or groups for whom petitions are offered in the prayers. Identify individuals or groups in

your own church or community for whom you wish to offer an intercessory prayer. Determine to pray through your list each day during the coming week.
6. Make a paper chain like the ones we make for Christmas trees. Cut strips of paper and give each person fifteen strips. Ask them to write an item for prayer on each slip. The concerns can be global, congregational, or personal. Make the strips into a large chain. You may take turns taking the chain home for a week, or place it in a special area of your church. You may also choose to take parts of the chain to each home. Remind group members that we are bound in a loving way to one another and to God through our prayers.
7. Take a prayer walk through your church building, praying in each room for what is done there and what God will do in the future there. You may also take a prayer walk in a hospital, stopping on each floor to pray. You may prayer-walk through a mall, a park, or a zoo. Be creative! The idea of a prayer walk is to be in intercessory prayer around each place you stop on the walk. You can do this in silence or in another way.
8. Create a litany of intercession. A simple litany of intercession allows time for individuals to offer petitions to God. The group responds to each petition with a simple plea, such as "Hear our prayer, O God."

5

God's "Chosen"
Amos 3:1-2; 5:18-20; 9:7-8, 11-15

Amos attacks the people's reliance on their special status as God's "chosen." Being chosen does not single people out as being better than others. Rather, it demands even more from the chosen ones.

Personal Preparation

1. Look up the word *iconoclast* in a dictionary, and then read Amos 3:1-2. What attitude or behavior does Amos attack in this passage? According to verse 2, what distinguishes Israel from other peoples?
2. Read Amos 5:18-20. What is the "day of the Lord"? Why might the Israelites look forward to the "day of the Lord"? Why does Amos tell them they should fear that day?
3. Read Amos 9:7-8. What do you know about the three non-Israelite peoples mentioned here (referred to as Ethiopians, Philistines, and Arameans in the NRSV)? If you have access to a Bible dictionary, find out more about these peoples.
4. Spend some time reflecting on what it means to you to be "chosen." Have you ever been singled out for a special purpose? How did it make you feel? How do you feel when other people are given special privileges?

Understanding

Nobody likes an iconoclast, someone who attacks our beliefs and ideals. How can we like someone who takes our most cherished belief, holds it in front of us, and pops it so that it collapses like a balloon? But every group needs an iconoclast: someone who takes the wind out of our sails when we begin to think too highly of ourselves; someone who shouts "But the emperor's not wearing any clothes," when we get so caught up with ourselves that we can no longer see or think clearly.

The Jewish theologian Abraham Heschel calls Amos an iconoclast, because the prophet takes some of the central Israelite beliefs, turns them around, and uses them against the Israelites. Each time Amos does this, he takes an honored tradition that people believe offers salvation and announces that it is the very tradition that will bring judgment upon them.

The Meaning of "Chosen"

In Amos 3:1-2, the prophet takes up the Israelite belief in "election." Election, the tradition that God has elected (chosen) to enter into a special relationship with the Israelites, goes back to the ancestors Abraham and Sarah. In Genesis 12:2, God announces to Abraham (then called Abram), "I will make of you a great nation, and I will bless you, and make your name great." Abraham and Sarah become the ancestors of the nation chosen by God.

This election tradition continued through the time of the Exodus. To the people leaving Egypt, the descendants of Abraham and Sarah, God says, "Now, therefore, if you obey my voice and keep my covenant, you shall be my treasured possession out of all the peoples."

A "great nation," a "treasured possession"—this is how the Israelites thought of themselves in the time of Amos. Consequently, the first half of Amos's message in 3:2 would have come as no surprise: "You only have I known of all the families of the earth." (The prophet here, as in other places, speaks as God's mouthpiece and therefore uses the divine "I.") I can imagine the Israelites looking at each other, nodding their heads, and saying, "This fellow knows what he's talking about."

The second half of Amos's announcement would have shocked the Israelites, however. "Therefore I will punish you for all your iniquities." At the conclusion of the prophetic message, the brows would furrow and the heads would shake from side to side. "How can this be?" the Israelites would ask. "How can election lead to punishment?"

Amos does not contest the fact that God chose the Israelites, but rather, he criticizes the way the Israelites have interpreted their chosenness. Amos says to them that being chosen does not offer a refuge from responsibility. It doesn't grant immunity. Rather, it makes the Israelites even more responsible. Being chosen means being held accountable.

Chosenness is not simply a feeling of being special. It is not a statement of favoritism. Being chosen means that God knows Israel, and Israel knows God. Israel's knowledge of God provides a basis for a new way of living, a new way of seeing the world, a new responsibility for creation.

The "Day of the Lord"

Amos also overturns the Israelites' expectations related to the "day of the LORD." The phrase "day of the LORD" and other closely related expressions occur over two dozen times in the prophetic literature. Simpler forms of this expression, such as "that day" or "the day when," appear nearly two hundred times in the Prophets. In many of these occurrences, the phrase refers to the time when God will defeat Israel's enemies. In 5:18-20, Amos turns this idea on its head. Because the Israelites have broken their covenant with God, they should fear "that day."

> It is darkness, not light;
> as if someone fled from a lion,
> and was met by a bear;
> or went into the house and rested a hand against the wall,
> and was bitten by a snake.

Things can't get worse—but they do! On that day, God will judge Israel, and like the person who flees to their house to seek refuge from wild animals, Israel will not escape the judgment. Election does not protect those whom God chooses. Election demands that the chosen live according to God's teachings.

Just as the knowledge of being chosen by God led the Israelites to regard themselves as immune from judgment, it also apparently encouraged some to think of themselves as better than other peoples. In 9:7-8 Amos attacks this "holier than thou" attitude. Again, Amos delivers an oracle (or message) directly from God to the people:

> "Are you not like the Ethiopians to me,
> O people of Israel?" says the Lord.
> "Did I not bring Israel up from the land of Egypt,
> and the Philistines from Caphtor and the
> Arameans from Kir?"

In God's eyes, the Israelites are like the Ethiopians, a people living far distant from Palestine, in the land south of Egypt. And, wonder of wonders, Amos declares that Israel's exodus from Egypt was not the only exodus guided by God. Israel's God also led Israel's enemies—the Philistines and Arameans—in their migrations! Being chosen does not grant superiority over other peoples.

Reactions to the 1991 Gulf War disheartened me. When the war ended, many U.S. citizens jubilantly pronounced our country fortunate. "So few casualties," they exclaimed. Few people seemed to give a moment's thought to the Iraqi soldiers who were killed in battle or the Iraqi civilians who died when U.S. bombs fell on their cities and towns. As the PBS *Frontline* documentary "The War We Left Behind" reveals, the damage we inflicted upon Iraq's infrastructure severely affected the health and welfare of Iraqi civilians—men, women, and children. It makes me think of Mark Twain's short story "The War Prayer." In it, a messenger from God tells a gathering of patriotic church people that their uttered prayer for victory had necessarily included some horrendous unspoken requests. This is what they had, in effect, prayed for:

> O Lord our God, help us to tear their soldiers to bloody shreds with our shells; help us to cover their smiling fields with the pale forms of their patriot dead; help us to drown the thunder of the guns with the shrieks of their wounded, writhing in pain; help us to lay waste their humble homes with a hurricane of fire; help us to wring the hearts of their unoffending widows with unavailing grief....
>
> For our sakes who adore Thee, Lord, blast their hopes, blight their lives, protract their bitter pilgrimage, make heavy their steps, water their way with their tears, stain the white snow with the blood of their wounded feet! We ask it, in the spirit of love, of Him Who is the source of Love, and Who is the ever-faithful refuge and friend of all that are sore beset and seek His aid with humble and contrite hearts. Amen.

Who of us would actually pray such a prayer? Yet we do often seem to have the need to elevate ourselves by putting other people down. Christians are not immune to this disease. Catholics and Protestants put one another down. One denomination mocks another. Christians disparage Jews or Muslims or Hindus.

Is it possible to feel chosen and *not* feel superior to others? Does chosenness automatically grant superiority? Or, can we feel chosen to experience God in a certain way, without viewing this experience as better than the experience others have? To borrow the Apostle Paul's metaphor—are Christians one member of one great body that includes as members all human families on our planet?

The Offer of Hope

As iconoclast, Amos continues his prophetic role as critic. We've seen how the prophet attacked the Israelites who oppressed the poor and needy in their communities. We've seen how he called for justice and righteousness to be practiced in Israel. We've seen in today's lesson how Amos attacked the very core of the Israelites' self-understanding—their chosenness. What about his energizing role? Does Amos have anything good to say?

Some interpreters believe that the prophet Amos offered only criticism, that his message was entirely one of doom and destruction. Nevertheless, the book of Amos ends on a positive note (9:11-15). The book offers hope. It promises *shalom*, a restoration of justice and wholeness. Although Amos may have spoken only of the impending judgment upon Israel, the individual who collected Amos's prophetic messages determined that it was important to conclude the book with a message of hope for the reader.

> "I will restore the fortunes of my people Israel,
>   and they shall rebuild the ruined cities and
>   inhabit them,
> they shall plant vineyards and drink their wine,
>   and they shall make gardens and eat their fruit.
> I will plant them upon their land,
>   and they shall never again be plucked up
>   out of their land that I have given them,"
>   says the Lord your God. (9:14-15)

In the midst of our despair over our human weaknesses, our inability to live in relationship to others as we know we should live, we receive a message of hope. We learn that judgment is not God's final word. When and how this new era of shalom will be established is not stated in the book of Amos, but these concluding verses lift our vision and urge us to open ourselves to the newness of life God offers us.

Discussion and Action

1. Share about times when you have been "chosen" in some way. When have you used your chosenness in responsible ways? Have you ever used it for special privilege?
2. Are there ways in which the church takes refuge from responsibility in its chosenness? If so, can you name some examples?
3. Spend some time discussing the idea of the prophet as an iconoclast. Can you identify any iconoclasts in your congregation, community, or denomination? What cherished traditions have they criticized?
4. Many times our lack of knowledge about other cultures, races, religions, or nationalities causes us to fear people who are different. Name instances where this has been true for you. What can your covenant group, congregation, or denomination do to promote better understanding between and among peoples?

5. The last sentence in Mark Twain's "War Prayer" reads: "It was believed afterward that the [messenger] was a lunatic, because there was no sense in what he said."
   Think about the kinds of prayers you often pray. How aware are you of the potential far-reaching consequences of those prayers—should God answer just as you have requested? When have you been thankful that God didn't do things the way you wanted?
6. Since this is the final session on Amos, spend some time talking about what you've learned. What critique from Amos do you most need to hear? What criticisms do you think the church needs to hear? Talk about ways to incorporate Amos's message into the worship and witness life of your congregation.
7. Ask group members to identify people in the church who could use extra hope right now. Find a way to offer kindness and hope to those people through phone calls, letters, or visits during the next week.
8. What did you find in Amos that was energizing? What part of his message gives you hope? How can you share your hopefulness with others? Perhaps write your own group message of hope—in a style similar to verses 9:14-15—speaking directly to some situation in your own lives, your congregation's life, or your nation's life.

6

No Faithfulness, No Loyalty, No Knowledge of God
Hosea 1; 4:1-3

Hosea's message resembles that of the prophet Amos; however, the two prophets differ in where they place the emphasis. Whereas Amos criticizes the people for their unjust acts, Hosea points to their lack of inward feelings.

Personal Preparation

1. Read Hosea 1 and 4:1-3. In Hosea 1:3-9, the prophet engages in a symbolic action by which he dramatizes his message to the Israelite people. How do you personally get involved in symbolic actions?
2. Read examples of other prophetic, symbolic actions in Isaiah 8:1-4; Jeremiah 28; and Ezekiel 4:4-6. Why do you think the prophets acted out God's message in these unusual ways? Think of modern examples of "prophetic symbolic actions" in which protesters act out their messages.
3. Read Hosea 4:1-3. How do you define "values"? What values does Hosea identify as absent in Israel? List three essential values you see missing in today's society.

Understanding

When we read the opening verse of the book of Hosea, we find that, like Amos, Hosea prophesied during the prosperous and relatively peaceful reign of Jeroboam II. The book of Hosea suggests that the prophet continued prophesying during the decline that followed Jeroboam's death. He may have even witnessed the downfall of the northern kingdom at the hands of the invading Assyrians, but we cannot know that for sure.

Like Amos, Hosea prophesied to the northern kingdom of Israel. However, his prophetic speeches seem to indicate that he was an Israelite (unlike Amos,

No Faithfulness, No Loyalty, No Knowledge of God

who left his home in Judah to travel north to Israel). The messages of the two prophets are similar: both criticize the political, religious, and moral behaviors of the Israelite people. Abraham Heschel contrasts the two in terms of what they emphasize. Heschel observes that Amos criticizes specific actions, while Hosea attacks the Israelites for their lack of "inwardness." We found in our study of Amos that a key word in his prophecy is *justice*. In Hosea, we find a corresponding emphasis on "knowledge of God," an expression which Hosea uses to refer to both a relationship with God and knowledge of God's teachings.

Hosea shows great creativity in his prophetic sayings. When speaking of the relationship between God and the Israelite people, the prophet uses many vivid images. A few examples will show the prophet's imaginative spark. In chapters 1—3, Hosea portrays God as a loyal husband bound to a faithless wife (Israel). He also describes God as a cattle herder and Israel as a stubborn heifer (4:16). God is a bird catcher, Israel a silly dove (7:11-12). God is a loving parent, Israel a rebellious child (11:1-3).

Prophetic Symbolic Action

In addition to using striking imagery in his prophetic messages, Hosea did something odd. He gave his children names that symbolize his prophetic message. In chapter one we read that Hosea named his children "Jezreel" (God sows), "Lo-ruhamah" (Not pitied), and "Lo-ammi" (Not my people). Each name symbolically expresses the prophet's message that God is about to judge Israel. This strange sort of behavior, in which the prophet acts out his message from God, can be found in other prophetic books as well. Isaiah gives his son a strange name; Jeremiah walks around town wearing an ox yoke on his shoulders; Ezekiel lies on his left side for 390 days and his right side for 40 days.

The unknown editor who collected and assembled Hosea's messages organized the prophet's sayings in a particular way. Messages of doom and destruction alternate with messages of hope. Immediately after reading that Hosea gave his children names symbolizing judgment, we learn that he renames them with names symbolizing renewal (1:10-11). In a message of hope, God announces that there will be a time when those people formerly named "Not my people" become once again "Children of the living God."

Faithfulness, Loyalty, Knowledge of God

What did Hosea view as the basic problem that would lead to Israel's destruction? Hosea 4:1-3 gives a succinct analysis of the situation in Israel. First of all, Hosea says, three important characteristics, or values, are missing in Israel: faithfulness, loyalty, and knowledge of God.

All three terms describe inner character and ways of relating to others. All three acknowledge a connection between attitude and action. By faithfulness Hosea means reliability, trustworthiness. Just as God relates faithfully to Israel, so, too, the Israelites are expected to act faithfully to God and to one another.

The NRSV uses the word "loyalty" to translate the Hebrew term *hesed*, which is a very difficult term to explain in English. Some translations use the word "love" or "loving kindness," but those words are not strong enough to express the meaning of *hesed*. To express *hesed* we must go beyond the notion of merely helping others. We must give of ourselves, being completely dedicated to others' well-being.

Hosea's primary criticism of the Israelites is that they lack knowledge of God. They do not know God's teachings or maintain an exclusive relationship with God. Because the basic relationship of people with God is broken, the relationship of people with people is broken. What can be found in Israel are swearing, lying, murder, stealing, and adultery. If this list of activities sounds familiar, it's probably because we know several of them from the Decalogue, where they are prohibited (see Exod. 20:13-15).

The picture Hosea paints of Israel is grim. People do what they shouldn't do. They lack what is necessary for survival as a committed community. It gets worse. Again, because the relationship with God is not there, the relationship with all of God's creation is out of sync. Hosea announces that the breakdown in the human community affects the natural world:

> Therefore the land mourns,
> and all who live in it languish;
> together with the wild animals
> and the birds of the air,
> even the fish of the sea are perishing. (4:3)

All Things Are Connected

In *A Worldly Spirituality*, Wesley Granberg-Michaelson observes that our western culture's view of nature is quite skewed. We tend to think of the "natural world" as something very different from "human culture." But a statement from Hehaka Sapa, also known as Black Elk, reveals a different way to look at things—as all connected, as in a circle. He writes in his 1931 autobiography:

> You have noticed that everything an Indian does is in a circle, and that is because the Power of the World always works in circles, and

everything tries to be round.... The Sky is round and I have heard that the earth is round like a ball and so are all the stars. The Wind, in its greatest power, whirls. Birds make their nests in circles, for theirs is the same religion as ours. The sun comes forth and goes down again in a circle. The moon does the same, and both are round.

Even the seasons form a great circle in their changing, and always come back again to where they were. The life of a man is a circle from childhood to childhood and so it is in everything where power moves. Our tipis were round like the nests of birds and these were always set in a circle, the nation's hoop, a nest of many nests where the Great Spirit meant for us to hatch our children.

Hosea also views plants, animals, and humans as interrelated parts of God's one creation. Consequently, a disruption in the human sphere affects the sphere of plants and animals. By rebelling against God, humans can upset the *shalom* of the world that is God's good creation.

The condition of our air and water on Planet Earth today suggests that we do, in fact, see ourselves disconnected from our environment. Despite warnings that we are making our world uninhabitable, we continue blithely in ways that cause our land to mourn and our wildlife to perish.

There are some hopeful signs. People are giving up the use of plastic foam products. Parents are switching to cloth diapers. Consumers are looking for "green" products that do not harm our planet. Areas are designated for animals. Christians have begun to awaken to their responsibility for the planet. Books such as *A Worldly Spirituality* and Shantilal Bhagat's *Creation in Crisis* call Christians to reexamine their view of creation. Groups such as the North American Conference on Christianity and Ecology have formed. The World Council of Churches' Seventh Assembly focused on the theme "Come, Holy Spirit, Renew the Whole Creation."

Nevertheless, we are in a crisis. Will we take this crisis seriously enough? Will the Christian community recognize humans, plants, animals, earth as interdependent parts of God's one good creation? I wonder. If Hosea could see our dirty rivers, dying trees, and thick, gray air, what would he think? If he were to speak to the church today, what would he say? If he were to raise a family in this age of acid rain and a depleted ozone layer, what symbolic names would he give his children?

Discussion and Action

1. Talk about the three essential values you identified as missing in society today. Why do you think they are missing?

2. Biblical interpreters refer to Hosea's naming of his children as a "prophetic symbolic action." Talk about the effectiveness of dramatizing one's message in this way. Share the modern examples of "prophetic symbolic actions" you thought of in your preparation for this session.
3. Talk about ways your covenant group might dramatize a prophetic message you wish to communicate to your congregation or your community about the values missing in our society.
4. Write a modern paraphrase of part of the text or suggest the names Hosea would use to symbolize today's Christians in our world.
5. Name some messages of doom and corresponding messages of hope in your life or in today's world (similar to Hosea's names of "Not my people" and "Children of the living God"). Do you think the church today has failed to "act" properly, as Amos suggests? Does it lack "inwardness" or faithfulness, as Hosea suggests?
6. Talk about the quote from Black Elk. How do you view the relationship between humans and their world? How could our society benefit from a more "circular" view?
7. In his book Creation in Crisis, Shantilal Bhagat challenges the Christian community "to seek a fresh understanding of the relationship between God, humans, and the world." How can your covenant group learn more about this relationship?
8. If weather permits, move outdoors and give each person a one-yard-square area and ask them to find as much evidence of God's presence in that space as they can. Give them about fifteen minutes to make a list and bring back anything to the group. Have group members share what they found of God in that space.
9. Consider calling your denominational staff person responsible for issues of environmental justice and ask for study materials or suggestions for action. (The Church of the Brethren, for example, has a study packet on human health and the environment, developed by Shantilal Bhagat.)

7

Estrangement, Separation, Abandonment
Hosea 2:2-13

Using the metaphor of the marriage relationship, Hosea speaks of the estrangement that occurs between God and God's people. Even in our own lives today, we must become aware of the actions or feelings that cause us to become separated from God.

Personal Preparation

1. Read Hosea 2:2-13. How do you react to Hosea's use of adultery as a way of talking about the Israelites' separation from God?
2. Think about a time when someone you trusted abandoned you. How did you feel? Have you ever felt abandoned by God? How did you cope?
3. Reflect upon times when you have broken covenant with God. Decide whether you want to share these memories with anyone in your covenant group.

Understanding

Thomas Moore writes in his book *Soul Mates,* "When relationships end, not only anger but other strong feelings may stir." Hosea uses the imagery of infidelity in marriage to portray the anger that God feels when we abandon our covenantal relationship with God. Strong, almost violent, emotions surface in chapter two of Hosea. The depth of the divine pathos expressed in this chapter reveals to us the intensity of God's commitment to the covenant.

A Broken Relationship

In chapter two of Hosea, the prophet uses the image of a broken marriage to portray to the Israelites the condition of their relationship with God. In 2:2-13 the prophet focuses on the criticism. (In the final lesson of this book, we will look at the last half of chapter 2, in which the prophet energizes the people with a hopeful message.) The setting for this session is a court. Judicial proceedings have begun in which a husband accuses his wife of infidelity. The husband asks his children to beg their mother to abandon her adulterous behavior.

I have read this passage over and over again, and I am still struck with the violence of the imagery and the harshness of the language. We have no amicable separation here. A wife has betrayed her husband and the husband is desperate to get her back. Even the children are brought into the proceedings—something a marriage counselor would not advise a couple to do today.

As we continue reading in Hosea 2, we recognize that the picture begins to shift. Is the prophet speaking of a husband and wife or of God and Israel? Although the figurative language of husband and wife is never abandoned, we come to realize that the prophet is not describing to us a broken covenant of marriage, but a broken covenant between a people and their God. As we discovered in last week's session, the Israelites lacked "faithfulness, loyalty, and knowledge of God" because this basic relationship was gone. They were ignoring the instruction of the Ten Commandments by swearing, lying, stealing, and committing adultery and murder.

The Ten Commandments also taught the people to worship only one God, the God they knew as Yahweh (Exod. 20:3). From Hosea we learn that the Israelites disregarded the instruction to "have no other gods before me" as well. The adulterous wife in Hosea 2 speaks of her lovers. Who are these "lovers"? Most interpreters explain that the Israelites in Hosea's time were worshiping other gods, the gods of their neighbors, the Canaanites. The leading Canaanite god was named *Baal*, a Hebrew term meaning "lord" or "master." Hosea attacks the Israelites for betraying Lord Yahweh to worship Baal, a god who is no god at all.

A Suffering God

What moves me about this passage is the depth of emotion underlying the drama of husband and wife. More than Amos, Hosea lays bare for us the pain and suffering of a God who has been abandoned by the very people who had promised fidelity.

What will God do? In this setting, God has the right to divorce an adulterous wife. Some interpreters understand it to refer to the legal action of divorce proceedings. Others, however, point out that God as husband seeks to avoid divorce and to find some means of reconciliation.

In verse 7, for example, God as husband intervenes between his wife and her lovers in the hope that she will return to him. In verses 9-13, God takes even more drastic measures. If she does not return, Israel's abundant wealth will end; their public religious life will cease, says the Lord.

Many interpreters believe that Hosea 2:2-13 stems from early in Hosea's activity as a prophet in Israel. At that time the economy of the nation flourished (although, as we saw in Amos, not everyone benefited from the strong economy). To the Israelites reveling in their wealth and well-being, Hosea announces God's judgment.

I understand Hosea's message. I am moved by the pathos of his portrayal of God as abandoned husband. But I must admit that I am uncomfortable with the imagery. Why does Hosea choose the imagery of husband and wife to portray the estrangement of God and Israel? Why does the woman embody infidelity? Is Hosea implying something about the untrustworthy nature of women?

First of all, we can recognize that Hosea uses this imagery to pronounce God's anger with the Israelite *people*. He does not single out women as being more guilty than the men. We need to resist the temptation to reverse the direction of the comparison. Hosea portrays the people as an unfaithful wife not because wives tend to be more promiscuous than husbands, but because in the Bible, when God is portrayed as a human, it is usually as a male.

Second, we can acknowledge that the Bible has blessed us with many different images of God. No one image or metaphor captures completely who God is. Individual metaphors can reveal an aspect of the divine nature. Hosea's portrayal of Israel as the unfaithful wife and God as the abandoned husband reveals one aspect of the relationship of God and humanity. We must be careful not to think of it as the only, or even the best, way of portraying that relationship.

An Angry Bear

The prophets in general, and Hosea especially, draw upon an extraordinary range of images to describe our relationship with God. Family images occur: husband-wife, parent-child. Other familiar images occur: God as Sovereign, God as Judge, God as Creator. Hosea also draws upon images from nature to describe God and God's interaction with humankind.

Because Israel has forgotten the One who fed them in the wilderness, God says,

> I will become like a lion to them,
> like a leopard I will lurk beside the way,
> I will fall upon them like a bear robbed of her cubs,
> and will tear open the covering of their heart. (13:7-8a)

What a terrifying portrait of God's anger and disillusionment! As Virginia Ramey Mollenkott observes in her book *The Divine Feminine,* bears often symbolize stifling passions or illusions. In this passage the "bear cubs" stand for our human gratitude toward God as the Source of our very being. When we rob God-as-Mother Bear of God's "bear cubs" by withholding our thankfulness, God becomes enraged.

Two frightening images of divine judgment: God as the irate, betrayed husband and God as the angry She-Bear robbed of her cubs. It would be easy to turn away from these images and from the prophetic criticism embodied in them. May we instead face up to Hosea's message and turn within to examine ourselves. When have we abandoned God? When have we worshiped other gods? When have we failed to express our gratitude to God for all we have received?

We know that in the face of the call to complete faithfulness we do often fail. Perhaps it will help us to realize that our relationship with God is an ongoing process of growth in love and trust. I like the way writer Frederick Buechner describes it in *Wishful Thinking,* so I'll leave you with his encouraging words:

> Faith is better understood as a verb than as a noun, as a process than as a possession. It is on-again-off-again rather than once-and-for-all. Faith is not being sure where you're going, but going anyway. A journey without maps. . . .
>
> I have faith that my friend is my friend. It is possible that all his motives are ulterior. It is possible that what he is secretly drawn to is not me but my wife or my money. But there's something about the way I feel when he's around, about the way he looks me in the eye, about the way we can talk to each other without pretense and be silent together without embarrassment, that makes me willing to put my life in his hands as I do each time I call him friend.
>
> I can't prove the friendship of my friend. When I experience it, I don't need to prove it. When I don't experience it, no proof will do.

Discussion and Action

1. Share your feelings about Hosea's use of a broken marriage relationship to portray the Israelites' abandonment of God.
2. Try identifying with both of the characters. How does it feel to be the one who is abandoned? How does it feel to be the one who acts unfaithfully?
3. We have all acted as an unfaithful spouse in our relationship with God. Who are your "lovers"? What other "gods" do you worship? How have you broken covenant with or abandoned God?
4. How do you respond to the image of God as an angry She-Bear?
5. Talk about some other images and metaphors that could be used to portray God's sorrow and anger at being abandoned by us. Name first some biblical images—then others that are meaningful to you.
6. Do you agree with Frederick Buechner's statement about the nature of faith? Do you think "on-again-off-again" faith is the norm for most Christians? Explain.
7. Close your session by writing love letters to God. Or write a love letter from God to yourself or someone else in the group.

8

Political Infidelity
Hosea 5:8-14; 7:8-12; 8:1-14

Estrangement occurs when God's people rely more on political alliances and institutions than on God. Hosea's prophetic message calls us to reflect on how we make decisions as Christian citizens.

Personal Preparation
1. Reflect on your political involvements. How do your religious views influence your political decisions?
2. Read Hosea 5:8-14; 7:8-12; and 8:1-14. What imagery does Hosea use to portray Israel's political activity?
3. Think about the 1991 Gulf War and ongoing conflict/tensions in the Middle East. In such situations what does it mean to rely on political alliances and institutions? to rely on God?

Understanding

Do you remember how capricious friendships can be for children? One week you may be the center of attention among your friends, the person everyone wants to sit beside, and the next week you discover that somebody else has taken your place.

Our government appears to act at times with a similar arbitrariness. One year the People's Republic of China is out. The next year they're in. Iraq is an ally, then a demonized enemy. What happened, other than a presidential visit or a military miscalculation? Many of us who grew up during the Cold War are still trying to recover from the turnaround. For years there was a wall. Then, one day, it fell down.

Vacillating Nationally

Hosea criticizes the Israelites for a similar sort of vacillation on the national and international political scenes. After Jeroboam II's death, Israel experienced tremendous political upheaval. The security of Jeroboam's reign ended with that king's death.

On the international level, the Assyrian empire, which had been occupied with business in other areas of the world during the first half of the century, turned its attention to Syria, Israel, Judah, and Philistia. Under the reign of Tiglath-Pileser III, who came to power at about the time of Jeroboam's death, Assyria looked westward in the direction of Israel and thought, Expansion!

On the domestic level, Israel experienced political divisions and unrest in the form of coups and assassinations. Jeroboam's son, Zechariah, ruled only six months before being assassinated by Shallum. And Shallum was quickly succeeded by his assassin, Menahem.

King Menahem is perhaps best remembered for his pro-Assyrian policy. According to 2 Kings 15:19, Menahem paid tribute to the Assyrians. In exchange, they allowed him to remain as king.

Although Menahem managed to hang on to the kingship for ten years before dying a natural death, his son Pekahiah was not as fortunate. Pekahiah reigned for a mere two years before being assassinated by one of his aides, a man named Pekah.

Pekah reversed Menahem's pro-Assyrian policy, and, in alliance with King Rezin of Damascus, Pekah attempted to rebel against Assyrian control. This resistance resulted in Tiglath-Pileser's invasion of Israel, at which time he took control of much of what had once belonged to Israel.

Into such a time of turmoil and rapid change comes the prophetic word! Hosea sharply criticizes the Israelite leaders for their attempt to achieve security through political alliances. He takes upon himself the role of watchman and blows the trumpet to alert the people of the impending danger (5:8). Although Hosea's use of imagery makes it difficult to connect his sayings with specific events, most interpreters believe that he criticizes Pekah's alliance with King Rezin in 5:11, "Ephraim is oppressed, crushed in judgment, because he was determined to go after vanity" (that is, after a useless alliance with Rezin).

Assassination ended Pekah's reign, and his murderer, Hoshea, took Pekah's place on the throne as the last king of Israel. Hoshea initially exhibited his loyalty to Assyria by paying tribute to Shalmaneser V, Tiglath-Pileser's successor. Within a few years, however, he turned to Egypt for support and rebelled against Shalmaneser.

Again Hosea attacks the king's vacillation, this time between Assyria and Egypt, as he announces, "Ephraim has become like a dove, silly and without sense; they call upon Egypt, they go to Assyria" (7:11). In more general terms, Hosea castigates the nation for turning to other nations rather than to God for support:

> Ephraim mixes himself with the peoples;
> Ephraim is a cake not turned.
> Foreigners devour his strength,
> but he does not know it. (7:8-9)

Reaping Futility

Underlying Hosea's criticism of Israel's foreign policy is the understanding that Israel's leaders have broken their covenantal relationship with God. They have relied on empty alliances with foreign nations rather than on their covenant partner.

As a consequence of their infidelity, Israel will experience economic futility and eventual invasion:

> For they sow the wind,
> and they shall reap the whirlwind.
> The standing grain has no heads,
> it shall yield no meal;
> if it were to yield,
> foreigners would devour it.
> Israel is swallowed up;
> now they are among the nations
> as a useless vessel. (8:7-8)

Shalmaneser suppressed Israel's revolt by imprisoning Hoshea and besieging Samaria. After a three-year siege, Samaria fell to the Assyrian forces. The fall of the capital city marked the end of Israel's existence as an independent nation.

If you love history or politics, you may find all this interesting. But much of Hosea's political message gets shoved aside, because most people who read the Bible are looking for spiritual insights, not political observations.

Reading Politically

Does Hosea's political criticism have any relevance for the church today? In his book *The Bible in Politics: How to Read the Bible Politically*, Richard Bauckham points out the political dimension of the Bible. At the same time, he warns that we must tread cautiously when attempting to apply the Bible's political observations to today. We must be aware of the differences between the political contexts in which the Bible was written and those of our own time.

Very generally, however, we learn from Hosea's message that we cannot separate the political and the religious realms. We cannot say, "Here I'm act-

Political Infidelity

ing politically, and here I'm acting religiously." A life of faith has everything to do with how we live together as children of God, including the political aspects of life.

I remember that during the early months of the 1991 Gulf War, yellow ribbons came to symbolize this relationship of politics and faith. People who usually had little interest in politics displayed ribbons to show patriotism, support, and concern for U.S. policy. Those who usually cannot stand the drone of bad tidings on the evening news were suddenly glued to the round-the-clock reports from the Gulf. Business people, military personnel, politicians, and ordinary citizens had personal interest in the outcome.

At the same time, there was a surge of religious feeling around the country. Many found new importance in faith as they faced loss or even death. Conversions were common. Military chaplains were busy. Churches kept vigils. Pastors preached about the war, and churches displayed yellow ribbons on their signposts and meetinghouse doors.

Like the crisis in Israel, it was a crisis that made us see the relationship in life of politics and faith. When we are pressed to the wall, we see that God is relevant in our political as well as our religious choices, which, in a way, is symbolized by the yellow ribbon.

We rejoice with Hosea for newfound faith, and we weep for the God we abandoned until we face death and destruction. Most of all, we hope that faith will lead us and not merely be a response. It is not easy, in Hosea's day or in our own, to rely on God rather than on national and political alliances. It is a difficult task to know the meaning of being "in the world, but not of it." But that is what we are called to do.

Discussion and Action

1. Share some of your reflections on the relationship of politics and religion in your life.
2. Name some times or situations in which it is easier to depend on national or political strength than on God's strength. Share names and stories of people who have chosen God's way in such critical times.
3. Discuss how you as a Christian, or as a Christian community, decide how to act in situations related to church and nation.
4. Richard Bauckham observes, "None of it [the Old Testament] applies directly to us, as instructions, but all of it is relevant to us, as instructive." In what ways do you see Hosea's message as instructive for today?

5. What position does your denomination take on the Christian's involvement in politics? If your denomination has a published statement on this topic, get a copy for your group to consider.
6. Who are typically identified as enemies of your country today? What do you know about the lives of these people? Try to find out five things you do not know about them this week. Consider how this knowledge changes your perception of this group.

9

God's Compassion
Hosea 11:1-11

Hosea uses the parent-child metaphor to describe how God grieves when people rebel. The prophet offers us hope with the assurance that God will not give up on us.

Personal Preparation

1. Recall some of your childhood experiences. Did you ever rebel against your parents? If so, what caused you to rebel? Did reconciliation come about with your parents?
2. Read Hosea 11:1-11. Reflect on these words in light of your childhood memories. Reread this text throughout the week, memorizing it if possible.
3. Reflect on your experience as a parent or as one who nurtures others. How have you felt when your love was rejected?

Understanding

After Zachary was born, my mother looked at me and at her grandchild and said, "When you have a child, you understand how much your parents loved you." My mother is right, of course. The intense love of a parent for a child is unlike any other form of love. And having a child has seemed to give me a better, deeper understanding of God's love for me, too.

A Rebellious Child

In chapter 11 of Hosea, the prophet communicates a message from God to the Israelites. In this prophetic oracle, God is pictured as a parent and the Israelites are portrayed as a rebellious child.

The passage can be divided into four units. In the first unit (11:1-4), God speaks as a parent and describes the care given to the child. God says, "I loved him, I taught him to walk, I held him, I fed him." What did the child do? Ignored his parent.

"Out of Egypt I called my son." Here Hosea refers to the Exodus from Egypt when God liberated the enslaved Israelites from bondage. How did they respond to God's gracious act of liberation? They abandoned God and turned to worship other deities. In the first unit, the pronoun "I" is emphasized. In the second unit (11:5-7), the pronoun "they" predominates, and the speech shifts to a description of what will happen to Israel. They will return to Egypt. Many interpreters understand this to refer to the actual historical situation in Hosea's time. Because of the threat of Assyria, some Israelites escaped to Egypt.

In the third unit (11:8-9) God directly addresses Israel as "you":

> How can I give you up, Ephraim?
> How can I hand you over, O Israel?
> How can I make you like Admah?
> How can I treat you like Zeboiim?

Admah and Zeboiim were cities that had perished along with the infamous cities of Sodom and Gomorrah. The answer, of course, to these four questions is that God cannot destroy Israel. How could a parent destroy a beloved child?

A Question of Love or Justice

But what about God's justice? Amos proclaimed to Israel that they had failed to live up to God's demand for justice. Hosea announces that Israel has broken its covenant with God and that the effect of the Israelites' misdeeds will extend to all creation. Doesn't God's justice demand that Israel's people reap the consequences of their behavior?

No. God's passionate love for Israel exceeds even the divine demand for justice.

> My heart recoils within me;
>   my compassion grows warm and tender.
> I will not execute my fierce anger;
>   I will not again destroy Ephraim,
> for I am God and no mortal,
>   the Holy One in your midst,
>   and I will not come in wrath. (11:8b-9)

Hosea is not the only person to understand this aspect of God. The book of Jonah also confronts us with the human tendency to demand justice when God deals with sinful humanity. When God determines not to destroy Nineveh, Jonah flies into a rage. He cannot bear to see God spare the people of Nineveh. Jonah knows that God shows mercy to humans, but he doesn't want to see that mercy wasted on the enemy Assyrians.

Through parables, Jesus often taught about God's love. In the parable of the Prodigal Son (Luke 15:11-32), an older son reacts angrily when his father prepares a feast to welcome home the younger son. "What has he done to deserve your love? *I'm* the one who deserves the celebration," he complains. We are quite willing to receive God's mercy for ourselves, but we hate seeing it wasted on others. Can you think of a time when that was true in your life?

The Bible exhibits a tension between God's justice and God's love. If God meted out justice, none of us would survive. But if God continually forgives, we worry that some (not us, of course) will take advantage. We have all been the Prodigal's older brother at some time in our lives.

We can see this tension in Christian theology. Some Christians believe that sinners will experience an eternal torment in hell after they die. Others argue that a loving God cannot inflict everlasting pain on any individual, no matter what that individual has done. Still others emphasize God's love to such a degree that they believe that God will save all creation and that none will be damned.

A Second Exodus

Hosea has one last word in this prophetic message. In the final unit (11:10-11), he envisions Israel's return to God. There will be a second Exodus from Egypt. God will once again call them out of bondage. "'They shall come trembling like birds . . . and I will return them to their homes,' says the Lord."

I read Hosea 11 differently now. As a parent I can identify with the love expressed in this passage. Yet, one need not be a biological parent, or even an adoptive parent, to understand the experience of nurturing another human being. At the end of her chapter on "God as Mother" in *Models of God*, Sallie McFague describes the power of the metaphor of God as parent:

> We imagine God as both mother and father, but we realize how inadequate these and any other metaphors are to express the creative love of God, the love that gives, without calculating the return, the gift of the universe. Nevertheless, we speak of this love in language that is familiar and dear to us, the language of mothers and fathers

who give us life, from whose bodies we come and upon whose care we depend.

No wonder Hosea, the prophet and the parent, shows to us God's pathos (pity and compassion). Hosea has met the God who cares for children and yearns to bring them home.

Discussion and Action

1. Share about any instances of childhood rebellion that you recall. To what extent do you believe a child must rebel against parents in order to become a healthy adult?
2. Tell about your experiences as an individual who has been nurtured by others, both in childhood and as an adult.
3. Share your experiences as an individual who has nurtured others. How do you feel when your nurturing love is returned? when it is rejected?
4. Talk about your reactions to God symbolized as father. In what ways does this image express your understanding of God's love? Share favorite hymns or Bible readings that use the image of God as father.
5. Discuss your reactions to the image of God as mother. How does this convey understandings of God's love? What hymns and biblical texts express in helpful ways the mother image of God?
6. Reflect on the idea that we are willing to receive God's mercy for ourselves, but we hate to see it wasted on others. Have you ever seen this attitude in yourself? in your congregation or denomination?
7. Discuss your response to the prophet's message of hope and assurance that "God will not give up on us." Consider closing your session by singing the hymn "Softly and Tenderly Jesus Is Calling" (pp. 64-65).

10

Reconciliation
Hosea 2:14-23; 14:4-7

Hosea uses both the marriage metaphor and imagery of the natural world to describe the process of reconciliation initiated by God. Out of love God heals our relationship so that when God says to us "You are my people," we respond faithfully with "And you are our God."

Personal Preparation

1. Recall a time when you worked at becoming reconciled with another person. What actions brought about reconciliation?
2. Think about times when you have failed to heal a broken relationship. What actions hindered reconciliation?
3. Read Hosea 2:14-23 and 14:4-7. How does God restore the covenant relationship with Israel?

Understanding

In session seven we looked at Hosea's use of marriage to portray the relationship between God and Israel. We saw how Hosea pictures the Israelites as an unfaithful wife and God as an abandoned husband. Even though the prophets announce God's judgment upon Israel, they also dare to speak of the future in hopeful terms. Judgment is not God's final word. In today's lesson we read the rest of the story. Israel's infidelity does not lead to divorce, but rather, God's faithfulness brings about reconciliation.

In last week's lesson, we saw that Hosea describes God as a parent who cannot stop loving a child. In 2:14-23 God is portrayed as a husband who cannot stop loving his wife, even though she has taken other lovers.

In human relationships one person cannot bring about reconciliation. Both must want to restore the broken relationship, but at least one person must be willing to initiate reconciliation. One person must put aside hurt pride. One person must step forward and start the process.

Reconciliation

God steps forward to start the process of reconciliation with Israel. As husband, he proposes to "allure" his wife. Again Hosea uses daring language. The verb translated "allure" means to overwhelm or overcome the resistance of another. In Deuteronomy 22:16, the same verb is used to refer to a man's seduction of a virgin. The prophet Jeremiah uses the verb to describe God's ability to overpower the prophet's resistance (20:7). In our world we might consider such behavior sexual harassment. Yet, Hosea unabashedly describes God's behavior with this language.

God returns Israel to the wilderness. There, as husband, he "speaks tenderly to her." For Hosea, the wilderness represents the time of the newly established covenant between God and Israel. God, in a sense, is calling for a "second honeymoon" in an attempt to win back Israel.

In the wilderness, Hosea says, God will "make the Valley of Achor a door of hope." The Hebrew word *Achor* means "trouble," so that the place name symbolizes the reconciliation process that transforms trouble into hope.

All of this, Hosea reports, will happen in the future. We do not know if the prophet speaks of a specific day, such as the day of judgment, as many interpreters suggest. In any case, the prophetic message serves the function of *energizing*, which we learned from Walter Brueggemann to be an important role of the prophet.

As Brueggemann writes in *The Prophetic Imagination*, "The task of prophetic imagination and ministry is to *bring to public expression those very hopes and yearnings* that have been denied so long and suppressed so deeply that we no longer know they are there." Our deepest yearning is to live in relationship with God. Our deepest yearning is to live peacefully with our neighbors and to live at one with all creation. Hosea helps us to acknowledge those desires.

Hosea describes the reconciliation as a reversal of Israel's past experience. As wife she will know God, and God alone, as her husband. A new covenant will establish peace in the human community and peace with all creation.

A people who lacks "faithfulness, loyalty, and knowledge of God" will renew their marriage vows of righteousness, justice, steadfast love, mercy, faithfulness, and knowledge of God. Finally, Hosea's children, whose names symbolized the brokenness of Israel's covenant, will be renamed. "Not pitied" will once again receive God's pity. "Not my people" will once again

Reconciliation 49

become God's people. The kingdom that was to end (in Jezreel) will become a land that is owned by all the people.

Renewal

In addition to the marriage metaphor, Hosea uses other imagery to describe the renewal of God's people. At the end of the book of Hosea, the editor of Hosea's prophetic messages has placed another energizing prophecy to lead us out of despair.

The prophet begins with a call urging Israel to return to God (14:1-2a) and continues with a proposal that Israel approach God with a prayer of penitence (14:2b-3). The people's confessional prayer leads finally to God's promise of salvation (14:4-8).

A friend once advised me, "Give up the use of 'to be' verbs. If you don't, you'll never get out of your despair." When I think, I *am* a sinner, guilt and shame inhabit me. When I say to myself, I have sinned, I find the strength to try again. Hosea speaks quite a lot about human sin. But he says to the people, "You've stumbled"—not "You are a stumbler"— but "You've stumbled." And that makes it easier to get up and try again.

Hosea recognizes that we need confession. It is not enough simply to confess that we have sinned and then go out and sin some more. But confession, the public or private admission that we have stumbled, contributes to the healing process.

Israel's confession succinctly summarizes their wrongdoings: they have relied on foreign powers and on other gods rather than on Yahweh. Israel renounces this reliance on false security. The unfaithful wife discards her lovers; the rebellious child returns home.

God's promise of salvation begins with three "I" statements: "I will heal their disloyalty," "I will love them freely," and "I will be like the dew to Israel."

The first two images feel comfortable. God is the great physician who can heal even disloyalty. God is the faithful lover whose love knows no bounds. But the third image Hosea gives us feels strange to those of us who have grown up primarily with images of God as a person.

Hosea says that God is the dew that allows the people to flourish. Why do I feel so uncomfortable with that image? In the summer I walk out through my backyard every day to check on which plants need watering. When I see one withering, I rush for the watering can. When I lived in southern California where nothing grows without irrigation, I learned to appreciate the water I had taken for granted in the east. I would feel more comfortable with the image of God as gardener, one who takes action to fix things. But

Hosea doesn't call God "Gardener," he calls God "Dew."

Perhaps if we could talk more easily about God as "Dew" or "Air" or "Angry She-Bear," we humans on this planet would show more respect for God's creation. If we want to imagine our future into being, the future we hope for for ourselves and our children, perhaps we need to think of ourselves as flowering lilies, as cedars of Lebanon, as ancient olive trees. Then God could be the dew for us, and we would more readily sense our connection to all that exists.

Prophetic Energizing

Hosea criticizes and energizes. He shows us where we stumble and warns us of the consequences of our actions. But he also calls us to open ourselves to the love of God, who picks us up after we stumble. According to the good news of Hosea, this God is one who loves us with the passion of a husband, the intensity of a parent, and the fierceness of a she-bear.

Both Amos and Hosea represent the biblical tradition of prophetic criticizing and energizing. As critics, they speak out against the victimization of the poor in society, the abuse of justice in the legal system, the failure to observe God's teaching, and the lack of trust in God alone. They also offer us hope. Amos and Hosea affirm God's sovereignty over all human history. A loving God does not abandon us to our own folly. Both prophets challenge us to establish communities characterized by justice and righteousness. We do not live only in hope for the future; we also work at knowing God's realm and doing God's word in our lives today.

Discussion and Action

1. Refer to number 1 in Personal Preparation, and share your experiences of reconciliation with each other.
2. Where do you see a need for reconciliation in your personal life today? How might you go about seeking reconciliation?
3. The author says: "When I think, I am a sinner, guilt and shame inhabit me. When I say to myself, I have sinned, I find the strength to try again." Talk about ways you have called yourself or others names—names such as "the deaf," or "the blind," or "the opposition." How could you change these names to verbs or actions that would free up people to see themselves in new ways?
4. Hosea teaches us to expand our vocabulary about God. Talk about the images of God that have moved you in your study of Hosea.
5. Discuss confession as a part of reconciliation. How is confession important in your personal prayer life? How important is it in your covenant group?

Reconciliation

6. Talk about what you've learned in your study of Amos and Hosea. List the prophets' main points for us today. Think of a way to share what you've learned with your congregation.
7. Part of the role of the pastor in a church is to be a reconciling agent among people, sometimes between the congregation and community, sometimes among family members. Spend some time this week praying for your pastor(s) in this part of their work among you. Pray for your pastor(s) strength, wisdom, and forgiveness of heart. Make a plan to pray for your pastor three times a day and inform him or her of your prayer vigil during the next week.
8. Evaluate any outreach/witness emphasis or work your group has undertaken during this study. Will you want to continue this or choose another area of witness?

Suggestions for Sharing and Prayer

This material is designed for covenant groups that spend one hour sharing and praying together, followed by one hour of Bible study. The following suggestions will help relate the group's sharing and praying time to their study of *The Prophecy of Amos and Hosea*. You'll find session-by-session ideas and general resources for sharing and prayer.

The Reverend Cathy Myers Wirt has developed these creative ideas. Use those you find most helpful, and bring your own ideas for sharing and worshiping together in your covenant group.

1. Amos, a Prophet

❑ Brainstorm a list of current justice issues that are critical in your community. Brainstorm another list of justice issues that are on the front burner in your congregational life. How do you respond to seeing these lists before you? Do they seem like a list of opportunities for service/action—or just a list of hopeless situations?

❑ Share with each other about a time when you were in the presence of extreme poverty and a time when you were in the presence of extreme wealth. How did you feel in each situation? How long did you feel that way? Try to recapture and explain those feelings to the other group members.

❑ Amos reminds us that God judges our society by how the widows and orphans (in other words, the poorest of the poor) live among us. Who are the poorest folks in your community, and who is ministering to them? What can your group do in prayer and action for the poor during the ten weeks ahead? You might collect food or clothing for a shelter, make sandwiches each week for a feeding program, or create a quilt for a hospice or AIDS ward. Use your creativity and the resources at hand!

❑ Bring in a newspaper or current news magazine and cut out and sort articles into three piles: (1) news items about the wealthy; (2) news items about the poor; (3) news items about injustice. Which pile is biggest? What do you make of this?

Suggestions for Sharing and Prayer

- ❏ Choose one of the current justice issues from your brainstorming time above, and make it the focus for your group's prayer and action during the coming ten weeks. Decide on practical ways your group can express concern through service, prayer, and talking with others.

- ❏ Choose a prayer ritual or two from the list in the General Sharing and Prayer Resources. Covenant with each other to pray in this way during your ten weeks together.

2. Amos's Message: Justice and Righteousness

- ❏ Write letters of appreciation to people in your congregation and community who work for justice. Place the letters in a basket and pass the basket around the group. Ask each person, if willing, to offer a prayer of thanksgiving for the lives represented by the letters—and the lives these people have touched and will touch.

- ❏ Recall a time when you saw justice done and a time when you saw a great injustice done. Compare and contrast the experiences of the group, and talk about the different emotions that arise as you tell these stories. How do you know when an action is just or unjust?

- ❏ Remember the issues of injustice you discussed in session one. Focus on one of them and discuss: How would this situation be transformed if it were miraculously made just? What would be different? Who would change? What would change? How would *you* change? Make a covenant with each other to offer up to God your vision of a just solution each day for the next week. See how this prayer changes you and the situation.

- ❏ Sometimes injustice happens because the weakest voices are out-shouted by the loudest voices. In your congregation, who are the ones least heard? What insights do you have about this pattern in your community of faith? What prayer concerns arise from your observations?

- ❏ Scan local newspapers for stories of people who did acts of justice. Arrange these in a collage on poster board—and add to the collage each week. Use this artwork as a prayer center for your group. You could also offer it to be used in your congregational worship.

3. God's Upside-Down Kingdom

- ❏ Imagine that your home or your church building is the subject of an archaeological dig a hundred years from now. The place would be just as it is today. What will the researchers know about you and your priorities, based on what they find in your home and/or church building?

- List necessities and luxuries that you buy each month. How do you know what is essential and what is a luxury? Then list what a human being needs in order to live.

- Contact a local Habitat for Humanity project and ask about what they are doing. Pray for their work of securing decent housing for folks. If possible, offer some other assistance as well.

- If you are meeting in your church building, go to the worship space and observe how many things are in the room. Which of them are essential for worship and which of them are luxuries? How do you know? In your imagination, remove ten or twenty items from the room and imagine what it would feel like to have the room this way. Does it make a difference to you? Explain.

- Visit your local library and check out a book about Haiti. (The children's geography section will probably have several nice picture books on every country of the world.) This is one of the poorest of the poor countries in the world. Thumb through the book and pray for each person and family pictured. Pray for the towns and cities listed. How are the lives in your group like and unlike the lives of the people of this country?

4. The Prophet as Intercessor

- Share stories with each other about a time you prayed for another person over a long period of time. You may also choose to tell stories of a time when you know that others were praying for you.

- Make a list of prayer concerns, quietly or with music playing. Give people adequate time to do this—up to ten minutes. Place the lists in the center of the group and pray with your hands held toward the lists. Or you may choose to pass the lists around to read each other's lists in silence. If you are going to share the lists in this way, let group members know this before they begin writing.

    You may choose to send the lists home with people or trade them each week for the remainder of the study. Ask participants to place the lists on a windowsill or in some place where they can be bathed in light each day and easily seen.

- One at a time, invite individuals into the middle of your circle and lay your hands on them in intercessory prayer. You may choose either to allow the person to remain silent or to guide you in what you ought to pray about.

- Find a local Catholic church or outdoor retreat center that displays the stations of the cross. The stations of the cross are a series of fourteen areas for prayer that commemorate the walk of Jesus to the cross. Most Protestants aren't familiar with this type of prayer experience, but it can be very meaningful to do as a group.

5. God's "Chosen"

- Amos speaks of hope, but sometimes hope is hard to come by. How do the people in your group keep their hope alive? Share stories of times when hope was lost, when hope was provided by another person, or when hope was renewed after a time of hopelessness.

- Who is chosen in your congregation to lead? How do you choose your leaders? Pray for each church leader by name. Ask members to identify their feelings about the leadership they have taken in the congregation. What is it like to be chosen for the various roles in the congregation?

- The idea of chosenness is deep within all people. Most people see some folks as more entitled to life's goodness than others. Part of this has to do with whom we fear. Have group members make lists of the types of people that cause them fear or about whom they know very little. You do not have to share these lists. You may instead place them face down on a table and pray for your group's healing of these fears.

- Many of us find it difficult to stay hopeful on the anniversary of a death or a tragedy in our lives. Invite group members to identify these hard days. Make a list of them and give the list to each person. Discuss how you can be present for each other at those times during the remainder of your meeting time.

6. No Faithfulness, No Loyalty, No Knowledge of God

- Share the meaning of your name, if you know it. How did you happen to end up with the name you have? Include nicknames in your discussion.

- Get out a church directory and make a list of all the people in your congregation who are currently married. In your group pray for each marriage by name.

- ❏ Hosea describes God as a faithless wife, bird catcher, dove, parent, child. What image is most meaningful to you? Draw a picture of the image(s) of God that matters most to you.

- ❏ Use Hosea 14:4 as a "breath prayer," praying together in silence or with quiet music in the background. Say these phrases aloud together or silently at an individual pace:

    Breathing in: *I will heal your faithlessness.*
    Breathing out: *I will love you freely.*

    Remind one another that God is as close to us as our breath. And God's word renews our hearts, minds, and bodies, just as oxygen renews our bodies.

- ❏ Loyalty is an important value. Tell about the institutions and people whom you feel are loyal to you and to whom you feel loyal. Use group members' responses in prayers of thanksgiving as you close your session.

7. Estrangement, Separation, Abandonment

- ❏ Imagine some "wonderful" marriages you have known. Also spend some time remembering marriages that you believe were "awful." Make a list of differences. What is essential to a good marriage, and what makes a marriage difficult?

- ❏ Using the list above, can you identify in your relationship with God any of the qualities of a good and bad marriage?

- ❏ Betrayal is a theme in this section of scripture. Make a list of words associated with betrayal. Using the list of words, create a crossword-type puzzle on a sheet of paper, making the point that betrayal is a many-faceted experience and has many connecting parts. Healing betrayal is often difficult because the parts of the experience need to be sorted to be healed. Use this visual aide as a focus for prayer for your group.

- ❏ Share stories of betrayal experiences from which group members believe they have been healed. How did the healing take place? Note: Don't force this type of sharing, but simply invite responses. Ask group members to speak in generalities, if the situations are current.

- ❏ God never leaves us, and nothing can separate us from God. Many hymns reflect this sentiment. Tell about the hymns that assure you personally of

God's continuing presence. If the group is musical at all, sing some of these hymns together.

- Have a time of prayers of presence. During a period of silence (or while soft music is playing), imagine yourself in the presence of a warm light. Envision this light bathing you and surrounding you. Resting in that light and keeping minds focused on a scripture about God's presence or love can be a renewing experience. This type of "being with God," without demand or expectation, is like sitting with a friend with whom you do not need to speak in order to be in communion.

8. Political Infidelity

- When you were growing up, what countries were you taught to think of as enemies of our country? How has this changed in your lifetime? How do you interpret these changes?

- What war or conflict do you most remember and respond to emotionally? Tell stories about the impact of that war on your life.

- On a note card, write the name of one person or group of people whom you have known as "enemy" at some time. Arrange the note cards of all group members in a design on the worship center. Take turns, as people are comfortable, sharing prayers for understanding, forgiveness, compassion, and patience. God changes our hearts and those of our enemies one day at a time.

- How do the people in your group understand Jesus' call to love our enemies? Have everyone consider what it means, in practical terms, to love our enemies in our daily lives.

- If group trust is high enough, and the discussion can be entered without degenerating into gossip, name some times in the history and life of your congregation when people have acted as enemies toward one another. How were those situations resolved? How can your group help to reconcile people in unhealed relationships?

9. God's Compassion

- In silence or with soft music, use "resting image prayer" to imagine being rocked in the arms of God, just as a parent rocks a child.

- ❏ Bring in pictures of yourself as a child. Share significant childhood events and see if any of these experiences relate to how, as an adult, you understand God today.

- ❏ Pass a mirror around your group circle, and ask each person to say into their reflection, "You are beloved by God who made you." Invite volunteers to tell what this experience opened in their hearts and minds.

- ❏ We often use the phrase "child of God" to describe ourselves in the church. What is the difference in being an infant child of God, young child of God, adolescent child of God, or adult child of God? When you hear the phrase "child of God," what is your image of that concept?

- ❏ Look through your hymnal for songs that portray people as children of God and/or God as a parent. Read through the words and learn how the lyrics inform about who people are and who God is in relationship to humanity.

10. Reconciliation

- ❏ This is the end of a ten-week study, so think of ways to bring some form of closure to this session. You may write thank-you notes to each person for the gift of the past ten weeks, light ten candles of celebration for ten weeks of prayer together, spend some time sharing your favorite moments in the group during the past ten weeks, or find some way to celebrate your new learnings together.

- ❏ Take this opportunity to envision two people who are presently estranged. Imagine Jesus standing between these to parties, reaching out in both directions. Hold that image in your mind for several minutes. After some time of silence, share insights from this imaging experience.

- ❏ Take turns describing the biggest acts of forgiveness you have ever witnessed. What did you learn about yourself and/or God from these experiences?

- ❏ If physically able, play a game of tug-of-war (in good spirit), and feel what it is like to be in a "stressful" relationship. How is this tugging like and unlike a stressed relationship you are aware of? Do you see ways to reduce the tension in the relationship?

- ❏ Give each person a gift of love in this final session. Write each person's name on a large card and pass all the cards around the group. Each person can write words of love and affirmation on each card. Take the cards home to serve as a remembrance of your time together.

General Sharing and Prayer Resources

Forming a Covenant Group

Covenant Expectations
Covenant-making is significant throughout the biblical story. God made covenants with Noah, Abraham, and Moses. Jeremiah spoke about God making a covenant with the people, "written on the heart." In the New Testament, Jesus was identified as the mediator of the New Covenant, and the early believers lived out of covenant relationships. Throughout history people have lived in covenant relationship with God and within community.

Christians today also covenant with God and make commitments to each other. Such covenants help believers live out their faith. God's empowerment comes to them as they gather in covenant communities to pray and study, share and receive, reflect and act.

People of the Covenant is a program that is anchored in this covenantal history of God's people. It is a network of covenantal relationships. Denominations, districts or regions, congregations, small groups, and individuals all make covenants. Covenant group members commit themselves to the mission statement, seeking to become more . . .
— biblically informed so they better understand the revelation of God;
— globally aware so they know themselves to be better connected with all of God's world;
— relationally sensitive to God, self, and others.

The Burlap Cross Symbol
The imperfections of the burlap cross, its rough texture and unrefined fabric, the interweaving of threads, the uniqueness of each strand, are elements that are present within the covenant group.
The people in the groups are imperfect, unpolished, interrelated with each other, yet still unique beings.
The shape that this collection of imperfect threads creates is the cross, symbolizing for all Christians the resurrection and presence of Christ our Savior. A covenant group is

something akin to this burlap cross. It unites common, ordinary people and sends them out again in all directions to be in the world.

A Litany of Commitment

All: We are a people of the covenant; out of our commitment to Christ, we seek to become:

Group 1: more biblically informed so we understand better God's revelation;

Group 2: more globally aware so we know ourselves connected with all of God's people;

Group 1: more relationally sensitive to God, self, and others.

All: We are a people of the covenant; we promise:

Group 2: to seek ways of living out and sharing our faith;

Group 1: to participate actively in congregational life;

Group 2: to be open to the leading of the Spirit in our lives.

All: We are a people of the covenant; we commit ourselves:

Group 1: to attend each group meeting, so far as possible;

Group 2: to prepare through Bible study, prayer, and action;

Group 1: to share thoughts and feelings, as appropriate;

Group 2: to encourage each other on our faith journeys.

All: We are a people of the covenant.

A Litany of Mission and Ministry

For a clearer vision of the work you have set before us and for a better understanding of your gospel,
Lord, direct us.

For a deeper commitment in your service and a greater love for all your children,
Lord, direct us.

For a fresh understanding of the task before us and for a sense of urgency in our proclamation,
Lord, direct us.

For a greater respect and acceptance among Christians of different traditions and for a common goal in evangelism,
Lord, direct us.

From the Anglican Province of the Indian Ocean

A Litany on Reconciliation

Leader: If anyone is in Christ, there is a new creation;
everything old has passed away;
see, everything has become new!

All: All this is from God,
who reconciled us to himself through Christ,
and has given us the ministry of reconciliation;
that is, in Christ God was reconciling the world to himself,
not counting their trespasses against them,
and entrusting the message of reconciliation to us.

Leader: So we are ambassadors for Christ,
since God is making his appeal through us;
we entreat you on behalf of Christ, to be reconciled to God.

All: For our sake he made him to be sin who knew no sin,
so that in him we might become the righteousness of God

–2 Corinthians 5:17-21

Each Time You Meet: Some Prayer Ritual Suggestions

Prayer and sharing time in People of the Covenant groups is precious time. During this time the focus shifts to the more active and affective side of the group members, seeking God in one another and in prayer. Consider choosing a prayer discipline and keeping that ritual together for the full ten-week period. Here are some suggestions for prayer rituals:

Breath prayers. Repeat a portion of scripture over and over in the rhythm of your breathing—in and out. (See the example in session 6 of Suggestions for Sharing and Prayer.)

Resting in the music. Spend the first or last fifteen minutes without words, holding one another in prayer while listening to hymns or quiet music. You may start with five minutes and work up to a longer period of time.

Feet or hand washing. Because these texts deal with God's claim of justice and mercy, like flowing waters, you may choose to wash each other's hands or feet during each session. Begin this way, or send each other out with this ritual. You may also enjoy praying to the sound of rushing waters during your prayer time. Music stores offer tapes of these sounds.

Prayer walking. You may choose to do a "moving" prayer each week through the church building where you meet. Pray for those who use each room, the love of God they share in that place, and those who are yet to come to that place. You may walk the whole building in this way, or pray in a different place each week.

Objects of prayer. Each week collect items to give to a children's shelter or a shelter for victims of domestic violence. Pray for each item—and the person who will receive it—as the items are passed around the circle. In this way, you are dedicating your time to seeking justice in the lives of those whom you may never meet in person.

Candlelighting. Begin your sessions by lighting a candle for each person present. You will be signifying the presence of the Holy Spirit as you gather. Or you may light a candle in remembrance of a place where God's justice is needed in your life or in the world.

Newspaper prayers. Pray through the items on the front page of the newspaper each time you gather. Lift up the names of each person mentioned, and pray for God's healing and presence in each situation.

Choral prayers. Choose a hymn, chorus, praise song, or chant that you will use to begin or end each session. Sing it once loudly, once softly, and once silently in your hearts as you begin prayer time together.

Prayers for leaders. Pray in an organized way for your pastor(s). By doing this you strengthen the entire congregation. You can each choose a specific time of the day when you will pray for the pastor(s). Or take turns writing encouraging words of hope to the pastor(s) each week. Other possibilities include taking turns praying three times a day for a week, taking turns praying in the sanctuary during the hour before worship, or setting a specific time once a day when every member of the group will be in prayer for your church leaders.

Directory prayers. Pray for each family in your congregation by praying through your church directory, one family a day. Agree on the date to start and then send notes to each family the week before the day you will be praying for them. Let them know of your prayers for them!

Suggestions for Sharing and Prayer 63

Brothers and Sisters of Mine

Unison

1. Brothers and sisters of mine are the hungry, who sigh in their sorrow and weep on their pain. Sisters and brothers of mine are the homeless, who wait without shelter from wind and from rain.
2. Strangers and neighbors, they claim my attention. They sleep by my doorstep, they sit by my bed. Neighbors and strangers, their anguish concerns me, and I must not feast till the hungry are fed.
3. People are they, men and women and children, and each has a heart keeping time with my own. People are they, persons made in God's image, so what shall I offer them, bread or a stone?
4. Lord of all living, we make our confession: Too long we have wasted the wealth of our lands. Lord of all loving, renew our compassion, and open our hearts while we reach out our hands.

Words: Kenneth I. Morse
Music: Wilbur E. Brumbaugh
Copyright © 1974 Church of the Brethren General Board, Elgin, Ill. Used by permission.

Softly and Tenderly

1 Soft - ly and ten - der - ly Je - sus is call - ing,
2 Why should we tar - ry when Je - sus is plead - ing,
3 Oh, for the won - der - ful love he has prom - ised,

call - ing for you and for me. See, on the por - tal's he's
plead - ing for you and for me? Why should we lin - ger and
prom - ised for you and for me! Though we have sinned, he has

wait - ing and watch - ing, watch - ing for you and for me.
heed not his mer - cies, mer - cies for you and for me?
mer - cy and par - don, par - don for you and for me.

Refrain

"Come home, come home! You who are
come home, come home!

wea - ry, come home." Ear - nest - ly, ten - der - ly,

Suggestions for Sharing and Prayer

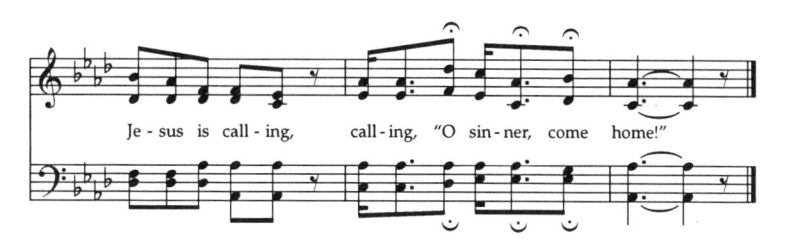

Je - sus is call - ing, call - ing, "O sin - ner, come home!"

Words and music: Will L. Thompson, 1880

Who Is My Mother, Who Is My Brother?

The Prophecy of Amos and Hosea

1. Who is my mother, who is my brother? all those who gather round Jesus Christ: Spirit-blown people, born from the Gospel sit at the table, round Jesus Christ.
2. Differently abled, differently labeled, widen the circle round Jesus Christ: crutches and stigmas, cultures' enigmas all come together round Jesus Christ.
3. Love will relate us— color or status can't segregate us, round Jesus Christ: family failings, human derailings— all are accepted, round Jesus Christ.
4. Bound by one vision, met for one mission we claim each other, round Jesus Christ: here is my mother, here is my brother, kindred in Spirit, through Jesus Christ.

Words: Shirley Erena Murray
Music: Jack Shrader
Words and music © 1992 by Hope Publishing Co., Carol Stream, IL 60188. All rights reserved. Used by permission.

Suggestions for Sharing and Prayer

Come and Find the Quiet Center

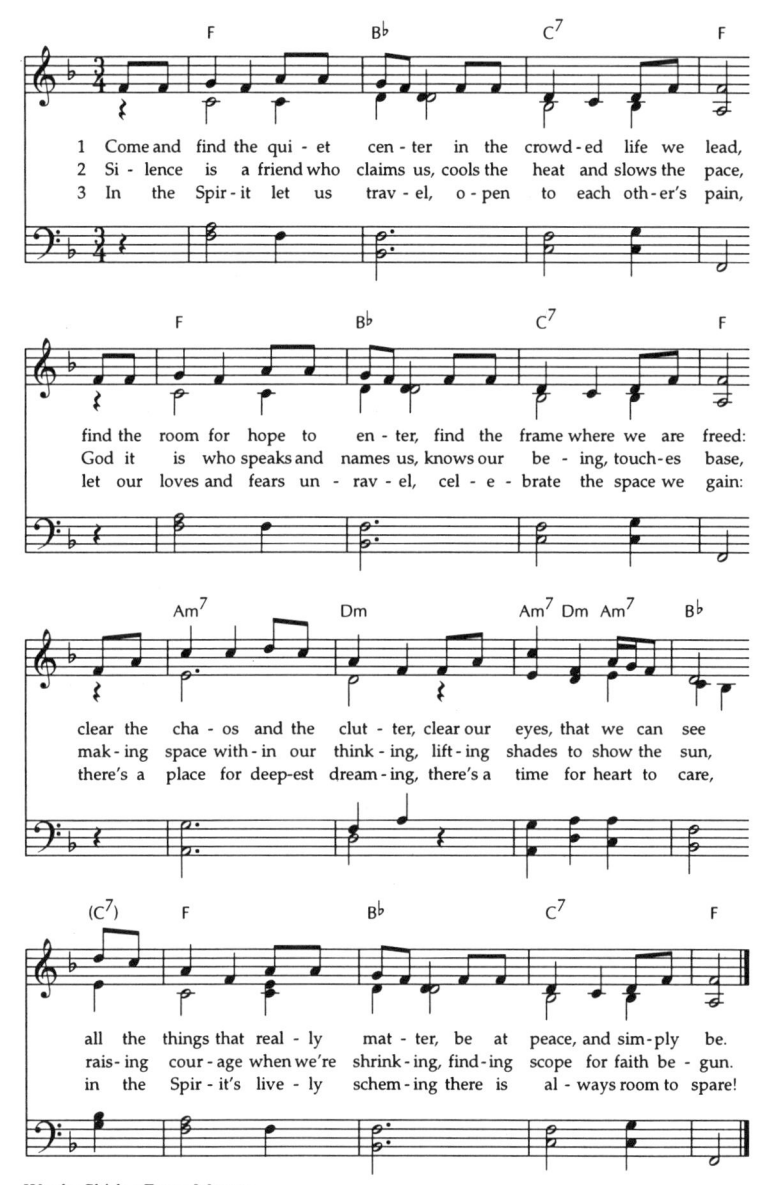

1. Come and find the quiet center in the crowd-ed life we lead, find the room for hope to en-ter, find the frame where we are freed: clear the cha-os and the clut-ter, clear our eyes, that we can see all the things that real-ly mat-ter, be at peace, and sim-ply be.

2. Si-lence is a friend who claims us, cools the heat and slows the pace, God it is who speaks and names us, knows our be-ing, touch-es base, mak-ing space with-in our think-ing, lift-ing shades to show the sun, rais-ing cour-age when we're shrink-ing, find-ing scope for faith be-gun.

3. In the Spir-it let us trav-el, o-pen to each oth-er's pain, let our loves and fears un-rav-el, cel-e-brate the space we gain: there's a place for deep-est dream-ing, there's a time for heart to care, in the Spir-it's live-ly schem-ing there is al-ways room to spare!

Words: Shirley Erena Murray
Music: Jack Shrader
Words and music arrangement © 1992 by Hope Publishing Co., Carol Stream, IL 60188. All rights reserved. Used by permission.

Open My Eyes that I May See

1. O-pen my eyes, that I may see glimpses of truth thou hast for me; place in my hands the wonderful key that shall un-clasp and set me free.
2. O-pen my ears, that I may hear voices of truth thou send-est clear; and while the wave-notes fall on my ear, ev-ery-thing false will dis-ap-pear.
3. O-pen my mouth, and let me bear glad-ly the warm truth ev-ery-where; o-pen my heart and let me pre-pare love with thy chil-dren thus to share.

Refrain

Si-lent-ly now I wait for thee, read-y, my God, thy will to see.
O-pen my eyes,
O-pen my ears, il-lu-mine me, Spir-it di-vine!
O-pen my heart,

Words and Music: Clara H. Scott, 1895

Suggestions for Sharing and Prayer 69

I Am Trusting Thee, Lord Jesus

1. I am trusting thee, Lord Jesus, I am trusting only thee;
trusting thee for full salvation, full salvation great and free.
I am trusting thee, Lord Jesus, my redeemer and my God.
I am trusting thee, Lord Jesus, to sustain me by thy word.

2. I am trusting thee for pardon; humbly at thy feet I bow,
for thy grace and tender mercy, for thy peace I trust thee now.
I am trusting thee, Lord Jesus, my redeemer and my God.
I am trusting thee, Lord Jesus, to sustain me by thy word.

3. I am trusting thee for cleansing, spotless in the crimson flood;
trusting thee to make me holy by thine own life-giving blood.
I am trusting thee, Lord Jesus, my redeemer and my God.
I am trusting thee, Lord Jesus, to sustain me by thy word.

4. I am trusting thee to guide me; gently thou alone dost lead,
ev'ry day and hour supplying graciously my ev'ry need.
I am trusting thee, Lord Jesus, my redeemer and my God.
I am trusting thee, Lord Jesus, to sustain me by thy word.

Words: Adapted from Frances R. Havergal, 1874
Music: Julius Dietrich, 1894

Other Covenant Bible Studies

1 Corinthians: The Community Struggles (Inhauser) $5.95
Abundant Living: Wellness from a Biblical Perspective
   (Rosenberger) $4.95
Biblical Imagery for God (Bucher) $5.95
Covenant People (Heckman/Gibble) $5.95
Ephesians: Reconciled in Christ (Ritchey Martin) $5.95
Esther (Roop) $5.95
The Gospel of Mark (Ramirez) $5.95
In the Beginning (Kuroiwa) $5.95
James: Faith in Action (Young) $5.95
Jonah: God's Global Reach (Bowser) $4.95
The Life of David (Fourman) $4.95
The Lord's Prayer (Rosenberger) $4.95
Love and Justice (O'Diam) $4.95
Many Cultures, One in Christ (Garber) $5.95
Mystery and Glory in John's Gospel (Fry) $5.95
Paul's Prison Letters (Bynum) $5.95
Presence and Power (Dell) $4.95
Psalms (J. D. Bowman) $4.95
Real Families: From Patriarchs to Prime Time (Dubble) $5.95
Revelation: Hope for the World in Troubled Times (Lowery) $5.95
Sermon on the Mount (R. Bowman) $4.95
A Spirituality of Compassion: Studies in Luke
   (Finney/Martin) $5.95
When God Calls (Jessup) $5.95
Wisdom (C. Bowman) $5.95

To place an order, call Brethren Press toll-free Monday through Friday, 8 A.M. to 4 P.M., at **800-441-3712**, or fax an order to **800-667-8188** twenty-four hours a day. Shipping and handling will be added to each order. For a full description of each title, ask for a free catalog of these and other Brethren Press titles.

Visa and MasterCard accepted. Prices subject to change.

Brethren Press® • *faithQuest*® • 1451 Dundee Ave., Elgin, IL 60120-1694
800-441-3712 (orders) • 800-667-8188